First World War
and Army of Occupation
War Diary
France, Belgium and Germany

50 DIVISION
150 Infantry Brigade
Royal Munster Fusiliers
2nd Battalion
1 May 1918 - 31 May 1919

WO95/2837/1

The Naval & Military Press Ltd
www.nmarchive.com
Published in association with The National Archives

Published by

The Naval & Military Press Ltd

Unit 10 Ridgewood Industrial Park,

Uckfield, East Sussex,

TN22 5QE England

Tel: +44 (0) 1825 749494

www.naval-military-press.com

www.nmarchive.com

This diary has been reprinted in facsimile from the original. Any imperfections are inevitably reproduced and the quality may fall short of modern type and cartographic standards.

© **Crown Copyright**
Images reproduced by permission of The National Archives, London, England, 2015.

Contents

Document type	Place/Title	Date From	Date To
Heading	WO95/2837 2/R. Munster Fus May'18-May19		
Heading	50th Division 150th Infy Bde 2nd Bn Roy. Munster Fus. May 1918-May 1919		
Heading	31st Division 94th Infy Bde 50 Division 6th Bn Roy. Munster Fus. May-Jun 1918		
War Diary	Latron	01/05/1918	01/05/1918
War Diary	Sarafend	02/05/1918	03/05/1918
War Diary	Kantara	04/05/1918	23/05/1918
War Diary	Alexandria	23/05/1918	25/05/1918
War Diary	At Sea	26/05/1918	31/05/1918
Heading	War Diary Of 6th Roy. Munster Fus. From. 1.5/18 To 31.5/18 (Volume 35)		
War Diary	Marseilles	01/06/1918	04/06/1918
War Diary	Racqueinham	05/06/1918	08/06/1918
War Diary	Courset	09/06/1918	17/06/1918
War Diary	Desvres	18/06/1918	30/06/1918
Heading	War Diary Of 6th R Munster Fus From June 1st-30th1918 Volume 36		
Heading	31st Division 94th Infy Bde 2nd Bn Roy. Munster Fus. Jun 1918		
War Diary	Racquinghem	01/06/1918	07/06/1918
War Diary	Val De Lumbres.	08/06/1918	16/06/1918
War Diary	Rouxmesnil	17/06/1918	19/06/1918
War Diary	Neuville	20/06/1918	26/06/1918
War Diary	Martin Eglise	27/06/1918	30/06/1918
Miscellaneous			
War Diary	Martin Eglise	01/07/1918	31/07/1918
Heading	War Diary Of 2nd Bn. R. Munster Fus From 1st To 31st August 1918 Vol 49		
War Diary	Martin Eglise	01/08/1918	16/09/1918
War Diary	Grouches	17/09/1918	26/09/1918
War Diary	Allonville	27/09/1918	28/09/1918
War Diary	Combles	29/09/1918	10/10/1918
War Diary	Nurlu	02/10/1918	02/10/1918
War Diary	Bony	03/10/1918	03/10/1918
War Diary	Le Catelet	04/10/1918	04/10/1918
War Diary	La Pannerie South	05/10/1918	05/10/1918
War Diary	Gouy	06/10/1918	06/10/1918
War Diary	Bony	07/10/1918	09/10/1918
War Diary	Reumont	10/10/1918	11/10/1918
War Diary	St Benin	12/10/1918	17/10/1918
War Diary	St Souplet	17/10/1918	17/10/1918
War Diary	S. Of Le Cateau	18/10/1918	18/10/1918
War Diary	Bazuel	19/10/1918	19/10/1918
War Diary	Maretz	20/10/1918	29/10/1918
War Diary	Le Cateau	29/10/1918	30/10/1918
War Diary	Robersart	30/10/1918	31/10/1918
Operation(al) Order(s)	150th Infantry Brigade Operation Order No. 192	03/10/1918	03/10/1918
Miscellaneous	Addendum No. 1 To Operation Order No. 192		
Operation(al) Order(s)	Order No. 7	04/10/1918	04/10/1918

Miscellaneous	150th Brigade	04/10/1918	04/10/1918
War Diary	150 Inf Bde T.R.I	05/10/1918	05/10/1918
Miscellaneous	Occupied by Items	05/10/1918	05/10/1918
Miscellaneous	O/C A D C D	04/10/1918	04/10/1918
Miscellaneous			
Miscellaneous	A Form Messages And Signals		
Operation(al) Order(s)	Brigade Operation Order No. 184		
Operation(al) Order(s)	150th Infantry Brigade Operation Order No. 196	10/10/1918	10/10/1918
Miscellaneous	March Table To Accompany Operation Order No. 196		
Operation(al) Order(s)	150th Infantry Brigade Operation Order No. 197	11/10/1918	11/10/1918
Miscellaneous	150th Infantry Brigade Instructions Forthcoming Operation No. 1	16/10/1918	16/10/1918
Miscellaneous	150th Infantry Brigade Instructions No. 2	16/10/1918	16/10/1918
Miscellaneous	B Form Messages And Signals		
Operation(al) Order(s)	150th Infantry Brigade Operation Order No. 199	16/10/1918	16/10/1918
Operation(al) Order(s)	150th Infantry Brigade Operation Order No. 201	28/10/1918	28/10/1918
Miscellaneous	March Table To Accompany 150th Infantry Brigade Operation Order No. 201		
Miscellaneous	A Form Messages And Signals		
Miscellaneous	OC. 2nd Royal	17/10/1918	17/10/1918
Miscellaneous	Messages And Signals		
Miscellaneous	2nd. Battn. The Royal Munster Fusiliers. Narrative Of Operations	03/10/1918	03/10/1918
Miscellaneous	150th Infantry Brigade Narrative Of Operations	01/10/1918	01/10/1918
Miscellaneous	Officers of Battn Present at Le Catelet Action	24/10/1918	24/10/1918
War Diary	Le Cateau	01/11/1918	03/11/1918
War Diary	Pommereuil and Fontaine Au Bois	04/11/1918	04/11/1918
War Diary	Fontaine Au Bois	04/11/1918	04/11/1918
War Diary	Forest De. Mormal	04/11/1918	05/11/1918
War Diary	Rue Des Juifs	05/11/1918	06/11/1918
War Diary	Fontaine Au Bois	06/11/1918	06/11/1918
War Diary	St Roch Chapelle	06/11/1918	06/11/1918
War Diary	St Remy Chaussee	06/11/1918	09/11/1918
War Diary	Sars Poteries	10/11/1918	10/11/1918
War Diary	Dourlers	11/11/1918	19/11/1918
War Diary	Taisniers	20/11/1918	30/11/1918
Miscellaneous	Officers With Battle Surplus Of Battalion	03/11/1918	03/11/1918
Miscellaneous	A Form Messages And Signals		
Miscellaneous	Instructions To Operations Order No. 18		
Miscellaneous	A Form Messages And Signals		
Operation(al) Order(s)	2nd Bn. The Royal Munster Fusiliers Operation Order No. 22	18/11/1918	18/11/1918
Operation(al) Order(s)	2nd Bn. The Royal Munster Fusiliers Operation Order No. 17	03/11/1918	03/11/1918
Operation(al) Order(s)	150th Infantry Brigade Operation Order No. 208		
Miscellaneous	150th Infantry Brigade Administrative Instructions No. 205		
Operation(al) Order(s)	Warning Order No. B.M 802	08/11/1918	08/11/1918
Miscellaneous	B.M 101	09/11/1918	09/11/1918
Operation(al) Order(s)	150th Infantry Brigade Operation Order No. 205		
War Diary	Taisnieres	01/12/1918	17/12/1918
War Diary	Le Quesnoy	18/12/1918	18/12/1918
War Diary	ETH	19/12/1918	27/12/1918
War Diary	Taisnieres	05/12/1918	13/12/1918
War Diary	ETH	28/12/1918	25/01/1919
War Diary	Curgies	26/01/1919	02/03/1919

War Diary	Wargnies-Le-Petit	03/03/1919	31/03/1919
Miscellaneous	Re-Organization Of Battalion		
Miscellaneous	Battalion Orders By Lieut-Col B.H. Purdon M.G. Commdg and Battalion The Royal Munster Fusiliers	02/03/1919	02/03/1919
War Diary	Wargnies-Le-Petit	01/04/1919	30/04/1919
Heading	War Diary 2nd Royal Munster Fusiliers. May 1919 Vol 52		
War Diary	Wargnies-le-Petit	01/05/1919	31/05/1919

WO95/2837 (1)
2/R. Munst. Fus
May '18 – May '19

50TH DIVISION
150TH INFY BDE.

2ND BN ROY. MUNSTER FUS.
MAY 1918 - MAY 1919

ABSORBED 6 BN 1918 JUNE
6 BN FROM EGYPT 10 DIV 30 BDE

FROM 16 DIV 48 BDE

ATTACHED { 31ST DIVISION
94TH INFY BDE

50 DIVISION

6TH BN ROY. MUNSTER FUS.
MAY – JUN 1918

ABSORBED BY 2 BN

2683

WAR DIARY
or
INTELLIGENCE SUMMARY.

(Erase heading not required.)

Army Form C.2118.

6th Royal Munster Fus...

Place	Date May	Hour	Summary of Events and Information	Remarks and references to Appendices
LATRAN	1st	1700	Batt. marched fm RAMLEH to SARAFEND dist 12 miles	
SARAFEND	2nd		Nothing to report. Resting day	
	3rd	1700	Marched 7½ m to LUDD Duning M/c at 1700 a the returned Officers horses sent back to Bgm	
		1445	Left in one clamp & entrained for an unknown dest.	
		1800	Men got tea at LC Jackson's Depot	
KANTARA	4th	0600	Reached KANTARA. Batt marched to No. 5 M.B.D.	
	5th	1530	Section orders to move camp	
		1730	Moved to Trans. Camp. 1½ miles off	
	6th		Paraded 0600 & 1800. 1630 to 1830	
	7th		Officers allowed in 3 men horse to visit	
	8th		Kantara	
	9th		Free to 1300. For went on line	
	10th		Battery parade 0600 & 0845	
	11th		Lt HAYES reported to post as ...	
	12th		...	
	13th		Battery parade. Co. returned at 1100	
	14th		...	
	16th		Capt WILSON ...	
	17th	0630	...	

WAR DIARY
INTELLIGENCE SUMMARY

Army Form C. 2118.

Place	Date	Hour	Summary of Events and Information	Remarks and references to Appendices
KANTARA	20			
	21			
ALEXANDRIA	22		HQ + D Coy Regt in train for PORT SAID	
	23			
	24		Remains in Harbour	
	25			
At Sea	26	1515	Sailed in convoy of 6 ships escort HMS PMalaya	
	27	1425	About noon sighted LEMNOS & CASTLE	
	28			
	29		Calm	
	30			
	31			

6 R. Munster

Army Form C. 2118

WAR DIARY
or
INTELLIGENCE SUMMARY

(Erase heading not required.)

C.R. Mundy's Tor

Place	Date	Hour	Summary of Events and Information	Remarks and references to Appendices
	May.		The undermentioned were admissions & discharges from hospital for the month.	
			Admissions 45 oranks.	
			Discharges 90 oranks. 6/5/18	
			83 " 9/5/18	
			51 " 13/5/18	
			40 " 15-5/18	
			1off. "	
			1 " 12/5/18	
			72 " 17/5/18	
			16 " 20/5/18	
			13 " 27/5/18	
			2off 367 oranks.	
			Ration Strength May 1st 2 officers 532 oranks.	
			" 31st 35 " 829 "	

C.Mundy
Major
Comdg. C.R. Mundy's For.

Confidential

WAR DIARY

INTELLIGENCE SUMMARY

War Diary
of
6th Roy. Munsters Fus.

from 1/5/18 to 31/5/18.

(Volume 35)

TC 39/19
94/31

4 Absorbed by 5/6/18 7 Bn on 5/6/18

WAR DIARY or **INTELLIGENCE SUMMARY** 6th Royal Munster Fus.
(Erase heading not required.)

Army Form C. 2118

Instructions regarding War Diaries and Intelligence Summaries are contained in F. S. Regs., Part II. and the Staff Manual respectively. Title Pages will be prepared in manuscript.

Place	Date JUNE	Hour	Summary of Events and Information	Remarks and references to Appendices
MARSEILLES	1st	0600	Arrived Marseilles, disembarked 1300 and marched to No 3 Rest camp. Nothing to report.	
	2nd			
	3rd		Bn marched off from Rest camp 0430 & proceeded to station finished entraining 0830. Left Marseilles 0700.	
	4th		Continuing with the train journey.	
ARQUEINGHEM	5th	0600	Arrived at ARQUES after detraining & marched out to our camp at ARQUEINGHEM. The 2nd Bn R.F. 2nd absorbed the 6th RMFus, with the exception of LT COL G PAGE D.S.O., CAPT & R.H. Offord M.C., CAPT J. O'Brien M.C., CAPT R.W. Chard CAPT E Gwer, M aro Steward, 2nd Lt J. Haynes, 2nd Lt R. Sheedon, 2nd & 2nd Lt Line, 2 J O'Donnell & 50 other ranks who were to remain as training staff to the Americans.	
	6th		Nothing to report.	
	7th		Nothing to report.	
	8th		Nothing to report.	
COURSET	9th		Training staff Lt.R.R. Burd 2nd proceeded to COURSET to attach commenced training 3rd Bn 319 Regt A.E.F. instructional classes & range practices recent classes & training	
	10th		"	
	11th		"	
	12th		"	
	13th		"	
	14th		"	
	15			

WAR DIARY
or
INTELLIGENCE SUMMARY

Army Form C. 2118

Place	Date	Hour	Summary of Events and Information	Remarks and references to Appendices
COURSET	June 16th		Nothing to report	
	17th		Usual individual classes	
DESVRES	18th		HQ moved to DESVRES. Took over the training of N.C.O.'s at COURSET, MENNEVILLE & DESVRES	
	19th		Training. Lt Col B Mongo offered ten of B gazetted N.C.O.'s	
	20th		Training	
	21st		Training	
	22nd		Training	
	23rd		Nothing to report	
	24th		Training	
	25th		Training	
	26th		Training. Capt J.E. Stiles left for England pending course	
	27th		Training. R.Q.M. on 2 line " " "	
	28th		Training. HQ moved to QUESTREQUES - hence over from 10th Dry Div. as "C" Group Training Staff	
	29th		Strength 30 8. 10 others. # 8 orderlies	
	30th		Nothing to report	

R. Offord
CAPT. & ADJT.
6th, (S) Bn. R¹ Munster Fus¹

CONFIDENTIAL

ARMY HEAD QUARTERS
INTELLIGENCE BRANCH

Dear Brown,
C.J.B. Records End
from June 1st 30th 1918
(Volume 36)

ATTACHED } 31ST DIVISION
94TH INFY BDE

2ND BN. ROY. MUNSTER FUS.
JUN 1918

WAR DIARY
INTELLIGENCE SUMMARY
(Erase heading not required.)

Place	Date	Hour	Summary of Events and Information	Remarks and references to Appendices
RACQUINGHEM	1-6-18		The training staff of the Batt. was today transferred to the 94th Inf. Bde. Company Commanders arranged billets for Coys.	(June '18)
"	2-6-18		Church parades were held today for Roman Catholics and Church of England. No other parades were held.	
"	3.6.18		Parade of all WOs NCOs + men under RSM and Specialist instructors. Employed men paraded 2.30 to 3.15 p.m.	
"	4.6.18		WOs NCOs + men paraded as yesterday. Coy Commanders were engaged on a tactical scheme with G.O.C.	
"	5.6.18		Parades as for yesterday. C.O. and officers proceeded to LUMBRES to witness demonstration at 2nd Army School of Musketry in a Coy in the field practice attack.	
"	6.6.18		The 6th Battalion Royal Hants Regt. arrived in RACQUINGHEM today.	
"	7.6.18		The 6th Bn. R.H. ? paraded for inspection by C.O.C. 31st Div. at 9.15 a.m. After this parade the 6 R.H. ? were absorbed by the 2nd R.M.? and too training staff.	
VAL DE LUMBRES.	8-6-18.		Companies spent the remainder of the day organising and cleaning up. The Batt. left RACQUINGHEM this morning at 8 a.m. and marched	

Army Form C. 2118.

WAR DIARY
or
INTELLIGENCE SUMMARY.
(Erase heading not required.)

Instructions regarding War Diaries and Intelligence Summaries are contained in F. S. Regs., Part II. and the Staff Manual respectively. Title pages will be prepared in manuscript.

Place	Date	Hour	Summary of Events and Information	Remarks and references to Appendices
VAL DE LUMBRES	8-6-18		to VAL DE LUMBRES. arriving at 3pm.	
" —	9.6.18		A brigade church parade was held this morning at 9.15 am. In the afternoon from 3pm to 5pm the Batt was engaged firing on the Musketry Range. Lt T. ROCHE & 37 ORs of the Transport rejoined from Base	
" —	10.6.18		The Battalion was engaged firing on the LUMBRES Musketry Range. Specialists paraded for training under the Specialist Officer	
" —	11.6.18		Firing on the range as on yesterday. When not engaged on range practices Companies & Specialists carried out individual training.	
" —	12.6.18		Range practices training as on yesterday. Coy Commanders attended a lecture on Gas Defence in the afternoon. Lieut Col. H.B. Johnson, Rev. DSO proceeded on leave to UK today Major B.H. Purdon M.C. assumed command of the battalion.	
" —	13-6-18		The battalion paraded for arms drill under the RSM from 7am to 7.30 am. 9am to 12.30 pm two Companies proceeded to bathe at SETQUES. Remainder of the battalion carried out Company training. In the afternoon from 2pm to 4 pm the battalion was engaged firing on the range	

WAR DIARY
or
INTELLIGENCE SUMMARY.
(Erase heading not required.)

Army Form C. 2118.

Place	Date	Hour	Summary of Events and Information	Remarks and references to Appendices
VAL DE LUMBRES	13-6-18		There was a lecture on to MERRIS attack this evening. This was attended by all officers and Sgt C.S.Majors & platoon Sgts. Capt A. KEEVIL 6th L.H. 2nd R.M. Bn has been awarded the MILITARY CROSS. Authy. London Gazette 3.6.1918.	
"	14.6.18.		The Battn paraded at 7 am under the R.S.M. from 9 am to 4 pm Companies were engaged firing on the range – Company training and testing of Box Respirators.	
"	15.6.18		The Battn. was ordered to parade to proceed to STAPLES. This order was cancelled by wire at 1 pm. The remainder of the day was spent refitting camp.	
"	16.6.18		Church parades for R.C. & C. of E. in the morning. Sudden orders were received at 4 pm to get ready to entrain for ROUXMESNIL near DIEPPE. The Battn left camp at 8 pm and was conveyed in lorries to WIZERNES where it entrained. Lt P.J. MURTAGH Army Cyclist Corps joined the Batt. for duty today.	
ROUXMESNIL	17-6-18.		The Battn arrived and detrained at ROUXMESNIL at 1 am and were accommodated in tents	
"	18.6.18.		To day was spent in cleaning up and refitting camp.	

Army Form C. 2118.

WAR DIARY
or
INTELLIGENCE SUMMARY.
(Erase heading not required.)

Instructions regarding War Diaries and Intelligence Summaries are contained in F. S. Regs., Part II. and the Staff Manual respectively. Title pages will be prepared in manuscript.

Place	Date	Hour	Summary of Events and Information	Remarks and references to Appendices
ROUXMESNIL	19.6.18		Boys paraded for training under Company Commanders. The Battalion paraded for medical inspection by Lt Col DALRYMPLE RAMIE of G.H.Q	
NEUVILLE	20.6.18		The Battalion marched from ROUXMESNIL to NEUVILLE and arrived at 3 p.m. 69 Ranks Joined the Bn. as reinforcements today	
"	21.6.18		Company training from 9 to 11 am. Specialists under Specialist officers. The Battalion paraded for Gunnis wave at 11am. Coy Specialist training was carried out in the afternoon from 2-3pm. Recreational training from 3 to 4 pm.	
"	22.6.18		Parade as for Yesterday. 2/Lt J.W. HAYES + 15 ORks joined the Battalion from 9 to 11 R T.M.B. Leave for this unit opened today. Rate to all ranks key day.	
"	23.6.18		R.C. Service at LE POLLET R.C. Church. There was no C of E Service. The afternoon was devoted to recreational training	
"	24.6.18		Parade of the Battn. under the RSM at 7 am for arms drill. Company training from 9 to 11 am. The Bn. paraded for Gunnis wave at 11 am. Coy training from 2 to 3pm and Recreational training from 3 to 4. Lt Col H.B. Torowdy DSO rejoined from leave today and assumes command of the Battalion.	
"	25.6.18		Parade as on Yesterday	
"	26.6.18		do	

WAR DIARY
or
INTELLIGENCE SUMMARY.
(Erase heading not required.)

Army Form C. 2118.

Place	Date	Hour	Summary of Events and Information	Remarks and references to Appendices
MARTIN EGLISE	27-6-18		The Battalion left NEUVILLE Camp at 2pm and marched to camp at MARTIN EGLISE arriving at 4 pm.	
"	28.6.18		Training as on 24.6.18.	
"	29.6.18		do — do — L.C. TARRANT rejoined the Bn today.	
"	30.6.18		R.C. parade for service in R.C. church MARTIN EGLISE at 7 am. C of E and Nonconformist parade for service in camp at 11.15 am. The afternoon was devoted to recreational training. No. 18364. CSM FURPHY 2nd R.M.F. had been awarded the D.C.M.	KfM

Thomas P Wah.
Capt 2/ R.Mun.F.
2-7-18-

Army Form C. 2118.

RY.

rmation		Remarks and references to Appendices
During the day having reached [...] the [...] to One thinner [...]RNETON-LE BIZET road. [...] Bde was severely wounded, Capt. [...] commanding 170th Bde RFA wounded [...]ASSEUR CABARET in U.16.b. [...] battalion front having a second [...]ing well in rear near NEUVE		
[...]dvanced their right [...] the line of the 93rd Bde HQ.		App. 480.
[...] have established 40th Div on our [...] in old British [...]16.d.		App. 481
[...] leaving property of EASTERN [...]		App. 482.

2nd ROYAL MUNSTER FUSILIERS WAR DIARY

INTELLIGENCE SUMMARY

DATE JULY 1918.
Army Form C.2118.

Volume No. 40

Place	Date	Hour	Summary of Events and Information	Remarks and references to Appendices
MARTIN EGLISE	1.7.18		Parade as usual. Quinine parade for the whole Battalion were hosted daily. Anti-aircraft guns were active during the night, no bombs were dropped in vicinity. Lt TARRANT assumed duties of Asst Adj. There were inter platoon trays of war football in the evening	
"	2.7.18		A Ceremonial Parade. Marshfield. Four new officers reported viz: 3rd R Munster Fus, Lieut H W Clarke, Lieut L G 13 Russell, 2 Lieut R C Kent, 2 Lt Nugent	
"	3.7.18		Battalion was on Camp fatigue pitching tents. The Asst Battalion Quartermaster & usual Battalion Parades & Camp fatigues	
"	4.7.18		There was a Ceremonial parade at 9.30 am. Attention was again called to the cutting of trees	
"	6.7.18		Permission was given for bathe in the River instead of the sea at Dieppe	
"	7.7.18		Church Parades were held. Inter Platoon matches were held in the afternoon. Fatigue parties were found for Camp Commandant. The Malarial expert Lt. Sir Daniel Ross attended Quinine Parade	

Army Form C.2118.

WAR DIARY
or
INTELLIGENCE SUMMARY.
(Erase heading not required.)

Instructions regarding War Diaries and Intelligence Summaries are contained in F. S. Regs., Part II. and the Staff Manual respectively. Title pages will be prepared in manuscript.

Place	Date	Hour	Summary of Events and Information	Remarks and references to Appendices
Martin Eglise	7.7.18		and Jocks to the men.	
	8.7.18		There was an inter-platoon marching competition.	
	9.7.18		Camp Fatigues. Lt C. Ryan reported from U.K. 2nd Lt Farrell joined from the 3rd R.M.F. and Lt C.J. Baldwin proceeded to U.K. Raided for the first time for a worth seventeen officers of the Battalion went the round of the Audruicques Dumps and docks. Treppe	
	10.7.18		Inter Platoon Drill competition and general turn out Lieuts J.R. Howe + B 1st Palmer returned from leave to U.K. There was a Ceremonial Parade in the morning and Recreation	
	11.7.18		-al training in the afternoon.	
	12.7.18		Parades as usual. Captain A. Keene M.C. to be awarded the M.B.E. June 5th 1918	
	13.7.18		Practice Ceremonial Parade at MARTIN EGLISE. Moved to N° 6 Camp in the afternoon and were kept busy putting it in order	

Army Form C.2118.

WAR DIARY
or
INTELLIGENCE SUMMARY.
(Erase heading not required.)

Instructions regarding War Diaries and Intelligence Summaries are contained in F. S. Regs., Part II. and the Staff Manual respectively. Title pages will be prepared in manuscript.

Place	Date	Hour	Summary of Events and Information	Remarks and references to Appendices
MARTIN EGLISE	14/7/18		Review of British Troops at Dieppe. The Battalion marched to Rieppet. They were complimented on their Arms work and Marching. The Army Commander General Rawlinson saw the march past at Martin Eglise on their way home.	
	15/7/17		Work on Hob Camp. Adjutant-General's Parade at ½ an hours notice. Capt. Livingston returned from leave. The Battalion became a unit of the 50th Division. 150th Bde.	
	16/7/17		Battalion employed on making new roads through Camp. Work 4 hours 5th man 2 Cribaulo in the morning 2 Companies in the afternoon. Captain T. Fry - C/plain late 2nd R.M.F. was awarded MC also the Word B. 2nd R.M.F. the D.C.M.	
	17/7/17		The interior of the tents were excavated to afford protection from anti-aircraft. 40 Lewis Guns were mounted as protection from aircraft.	
	18/7/17		Brigade Tattoos.	

WAR DIARY
or
INTELLIGENCE SUMMARY
(Erase heading not required.)

Army Form C.2118.

Instructions regarding War Diaries and Intelligence Summaries are contained in F. S. Regs., Part II. and the Staff Manual respectively. Title pages will be prepared in manuscript.

Place	Date	Hour	Summary of Events and Information	Remarks and references to Appendices
MARTIN EGLISE	19/7		Here was a Platoon Marching Competition. Parade as usual	
	20/7		Parade as usual	
	21/7		Church Parade.	
	22/7		Camp fatigues. S.B.R. testing in Gasshed.	
	23/7		Instruction of 30 yd Range in Wood. 2nd Lt Carruthers joined from 3rd R.M.F. 2nd Lt Nayler and McGuire were transferred to 150th T.M.B. also 1/2 of Coy. and seen.	
	24/7		Camp fatigues all day. The Rev R. Marsley Roman Catholic Chaplain was attached to the Battalion.	
	25/7		Camp working parties. The 30 yard Range was opened. There was a Reconnaissance ride for officers in the afternoon.	
	26/7		Parade as usual. Coy training.	
	27/7		Coy Parade. Tactical Scheme (Picture) Company Commanders	
			Irish Heir Platoon Commanders	
	28/7		Church Parade	
	29/7		Parades and fatigues as usual. The Right Hand Salute to all ranks	

Army Form C.2118.

WAR DIARY
or
INTELLIGENCE SUMMARY.
(Erase heading not required.)

Instructions regarding War Diaries and Intelligence Summaries are contained in F. S. Regs., Part II. and the Staff Manual respectively. Title pages will be prepared in manuscript.

Place	Date	Hour	Summary of Events and Information	Remarks and references to Appendices
MARTIN EGLISE	29.7		Came into force.	
	30.7		Parades as usual. Firing on the Range.	
	31.7		Parade as usual. Firing on the Range. Leave allotment increased to 15 men daily	

Honour
Lt Col
2g. R.F.
C'dg 2 —

CONFIDENTIAL

Vol. 49

WAR DIARY

OF

2ND BN. R. MUNSTER FUS.

FROM 1ST TO 31ST AUGUST 1918

Army Form C. 2118.

Original

WAR DIARY
or
INTELLIGENCE SUMMARY.
(Erase heading not required.)

Instructions regarding War Diaries and Intelligence Summaries are contained in F. S. Regs., Part II. and the Staff Manual respectively. Title pages will be prepared in manuscript.

Place	Date 1918	Hour	Summary of Events and Information	Remarks and references to Appendices
MARTIN EGLISE	Aug 1st		The Battalion was engaged in Musketry & Company training. Nine other ranks proceeded on leave to U.K. today.	
— " —	" 2		Musketry as on yesterday. Baths were allotted to the Battalion from 8 to 12 noon and were used by companies individually. Fourteen o'ranks proceeded on leave.	
— " —	" 3		Musketry and Company training from 8 am to 12 noon. Battalion Sports were held on the Brigade parade ground in the afternoon, commencing at 2 pm. Fifteen o'ranks proceeded on leave to U.K. today.	
— " —	" 4		Church parades were held in camp for C of E and in the R.C. church for Roman Catholics. Fourteen o'ranks proceeded on leave.	
— " —	" 5		Working parties were found by the Battalion today. Musketry practices also carried out. Fifteen o'ranks proceeded on leave. Seven officers joined the battalion today from the training staff of the 6th Royal Munster Fusiliers.	
— " —	" 6		The musketry range was used by the battalion today. All officers & N.C.O.'s attended a lecture and demonstration on training methods by Lt. Col. Livery 850. Five o'ranks proceeded on leave to U.K.	
— " —	" 7		Musketry practices and training under Company Commanders. One o'ranks proceeded on leave to U.K.	
— " —	" 8		There was a battalion route march today. "A" Echelon transport accompanied the battalion. Attack formation were practised towards the end of the march. Five o'ranks proceeded on leave to U.K. today.	

WAR DIARY or INTELLIGENCE SUMMARY

Army Form C. 2118.

Place	Date	Hour	Summary of Events and Information	Remarks and references to Appendices
MARTIN EGLISE	Aug 1918	9	Musketry, gunnery, and company parades as usual. Platoon Commanders attended a demonstration of a tactical scheme.	
"	"	10	There was a Divisional Field day to day. The battalion left camp at 3.30 a.m. Five O.Ranks proceeded on leave.	
"	"	11	Church parades for C.of.E. in Y.M.C.A. tent, and for R.C's in village. R.C. church parades by Capt H.B. HOLT and Capt T.P.M. INGHAM. D.S.O. joined the battalion today. Five O.Ranks proceeded on leave to U.K.	
"	"	12	Two Companies found working parties today. The other half battalion carried out a tactical scheme. Divisional baths were allotted to the unit and 5 were used by "B" + "D" Companies. The musketry range was used by Companies at different hours during the day. One officer and four O.Ranks proceeded on leave to U.K. today.	
"	"	13	The battalion carried out a tactical scheme and left camp at 5 a.m. The medical officer inspected the battalion by Companies in the afternoon. One officer and three O.Ranks proceeded on leave today.	
"	"	14	The battalion carried out a tactical scheme last night returning to camp about 7 a.m. this morning. Five O.Ranks proceeded on leave today. There was a detailed examination of Lewis Guns held this evening at 6 p.m.	
"	"	15	Adjutants parade at 7 a.m. The remainder of the day was devoted to Musketry practice etc. by Companies under Company Commanders. Three Companies found working parties of 4 hours each. One officer + 4 O.Ranks proceeded on leave.	

Army Form C. 2118.

WAR DIARY
or
INTELLIGENCE SUMMARY.
(Erase heading not required.)

Place	Date	Hour	Summary of Events and Information	Remarks and references to Appendices
MARTIN EGLISE	Aug 1918 16		Musketry practices on the range and training by companies went carried out today. Two other ranks proceeded on leave to U.K.	
"	" 17		Training & Musketry as on yesterday. One officer and 59 o.Ranks proceeded on leave to U.K.	
"	" 18		Church Parades for C of E on the Brigade parade ground and for R.C⁸ in the Roman Catholic church were held. Lt Col Jordan-Rye D.S.O. won jumping competition at Divisional horse show held this date. Thirty-two o.Ranks proceeded on leave to U.K. Transport of the unit was 2nd in Divisional Group. The Battalion found working parties and carried out training in Musketry practices, and under company commanders. Twenty four other ranks proceeded on leave to U.K.	
"	" 19			
"	" 20		Training under Company Commanders and on the range. 12 o.Ranks proceeded on leave.	
"	" 21		Musketry and company training. One company was engaged as work. Two officers and three o.Ranks proceeded on leave to U.K.	
"	" 22		The Battalion found working parties and carried out company training. Five o.Ranks proceeded on leave to U.K.	
"	" 23		Musketry and Company training. Twenty one o.Ranks proceeded on leave.	
"	" 24		Musketry and Company training as usual. Two o.Ranks proceeded on leave.	
"	" 25		Church parades as usual. 20 o.Ranks proceeded on leave to UK	

WAR DIARY
or
INTELLIGENCE SUMMARY.
(Erase heading not required.)

Army Form C. 2118.

Place	Date 1918	Hour	Summary of Events and Information	Remarks and references to Appendices
MARTIN EGLISE.	Aug.	26	The Battalion found working parties and carried out training under Company Commanders in Musketry Bombing &c.	
"	"	27.	The Battalion took part in a Brigade Ceremonial parade in the morning afterwards carrying out training as on yesterday. 20 O Ranks proceeded on leave to U.K.	
"	"	28.	The Battalion carried out a route march leaving Camp at 8.45 a.m. Battle formations were practised on the march. 15 O Ranks proceeded on leave to U.K.	
"	"	29.	Working parties and Company training. 13 O Ranks proceeded on leave to U.K.	
"	"	30.	Training in Bombing & musketry & delivering the assault. 2/Lt H.V. FLANAGAN joined Bn. for duty (28/8/18).	
"	"	31.	The Battalion watched a demonstration in drill under R.S.M. Oakley Grenadier Guards. Company training was carried out. working parties were found afterwards. 26 O Ranks proceeded on leave to U.K.	

Commdg: 2nd Bn. The Royal Munster Fusiliers.

WAR DIARY or **INTELLIGENCE SUMMARY**

Army Form C. 2118.

2nd R. Munster Fus

(Erase heading not required.)

Place	Date	Hour	Summary of Events and Information	Remarks and references to Appendices
MARTIN EGLISE	1st Sept		Church Parades were held as usual. Twenty four O.Rs went on leave to U.K.	
	2nd		Training was carried out as usual. Lieut Guerin went to leave to Australia and to struck off the strength. Twenty eight O.Rs went on leave to U.K.	
	3rd		Musketry training was carried out. A wiring demonstration was given.	
	4th		There was a Battalion Route March. 3 bivouacs who were left in camp. The march was 12½ miles. The men stood it well as if was the first route march since undergoing quinine treatment.	
	5th		Training as usual, bombing and musketry	
	6th		The Battalion marched out of camp at 1.35 a.m. and marched to Q.R.E. & F.S. where the Battalion took up a position to attack at dawn. At 5.10 a.m. a 3 minute barrage was put up, the Battalion then crossed the tape in 4 waves with 300 yards between each, the first 2 waves

WAR DIARY
or
INTELLIGENCE SUMMARY.

Army Form C. 2118.

SEPTEMBER 1919   2nd R. Munster Fus.

Place	Date	Hour	Summary of Events and Information	Remarks and references to Appendices
MARTIN EGLISE			Mass taken at 8.15 a.m. Another to be and bicycling to no taken at 7.30 a.m. The Battalion paraded about. Another mile and had Breakfast and had a church of 12.30 p.m.	
	7th		Training as usual. Brigadier Mount-Grane	
	8th		Church Parade were practical road to best weather. There was an interesting lecture to the boys of the army during the war showing what the army have done with regard to the Industrial house.	
	9th		Training as usual	
	10th		Divisional Sports were held at DIEPPE we to drive the way weather spoiled the Cattle's horse with the cup for the team bouts. The 2nd Royal Munster Fusiliers were not beaten by war too early won by the 1st R Mun:	
	11th		Capt Keerl M.G. took over Adjutancy of O By 8. Lieutenant A.M. Leave. Companies carried out field firing practice	

Army Form C. 2118.

WAR DIARY
2nd R. Munster Fus.
or
INTELLIGENCE SUMMARY.

(Erase heading not required.)

SEPTEMBER 1918

Instructions regarding War Diaries and Intelligence Summaries are contained in F.S. Regs., Part II. and the Staff Manual respectively. Title pages will be prepared in manuscript.

Place	Date	Hour	Summary of Events and Information	Remarks and references to Appendices
MARTIN EGLISE	12th		A divisional tactical scheme was carried out the attacking troops advancing from St MARTINS towards BELLEVILLE the attack was not carried out any further than that as the weather turned to bad. The Battalion was in Reserve Major Purdon M.O. in Command. Col. Jackson Rye was in command of the artillery.	
	13th		Training as usual. heather line. 2 R. Munsters Fus. beat the Northumberland Fus. for the Divisional Cup association three goals to two.	
	14th		Capt. Holt transferred from C Coy to A Coy there was an inter platoon transport shooting match for the Battalion association team near the R.I.F. but were beaten by the machine gun Company. The Fusiliers gave a very good performance in the evening	
	15		The Battalion entrained at 11.15 pm at ROUXMESNIL for DOUZENS D Company Cmne on next day. L/ Dodd was left behind in charge of Malarial detail Lt. F.O. Sewell went to Corps Rest House for a week.	
	16th		Arrived DOUZENS at 8 a.m. detrained and marched to RAUCHES	

WAR DIARY / INTELLIGENCE SUMMARY

Army Form C. 2118.

SEPTEMBER 1918   2nd R. Munster Fus.

Place	Date	Hour	Summary of Events and Information	Remarks and references to Appendices
GROUCHES	17th		Weather fine. Training as usual. Col. Von Rye D.S.O. returned to the Battalion having been away judging a Cavalry show.	
	18th		Training as usual. Company Musics were again tested.	
	19th		The Battalion had baths at LUCHEUX. Coy's the training as usual. 2nd Lt Sheffield went on leave to U.K. for a fortnight.	
	20th		Training as usual. Weather wet.	
	21st		Training as usual. The B.G. Burberry gave a demonstration at TISON FARM.	
	22nd		Church Parade as usual. A Lecture was given on the Operations of Yanks and Infantry by Capt Holt. Went to Bde as Liaison Officer. Col Rye and twice Officers of the 13th Hus. Came over and stayed to dinner.	
	23rd		Training as usual.	
	24th		Training as usual. Burberry field firing practice Parade as usual was carried out.	
	25th			

WAR DIARY or INTELLIGENCE SUMMARY

September 1918 — 2nd R. Munster Fus.

Army Form C. 2118.

Place	Date	Hour	Summary of Events and Information	Remarks and references to Appendices
@ ROUCHES	26th		The Transport moved to ALLONVILLE at 6 a.m. The Battalion 'bussed to ALLONVILLE at 11 a.m.	
ALLONVILLE	27th		Transport left ALLONVILLE at 10 a.m. and reached MAMETZ at 5.30 p.m. where they stayed the night. The weather was fine.	
	28th		The Battalion left ROUCHES in 'Buses for COMBLES where they arrived at 6.30 p.m. and took over billets from the 7th Queens. The Transport left MAMETZ and arrived at COMBLES at 2 p.m. The weather was stormy and the night cold. Battalion withdrew from Nurlu–Rye tent to COISY Battalion and Transport were billeted one mile west of COMBLES. Orders were received to stand ready to move at 2 p.m. at 9.30 p.m. more definitely proposed to 3rd.	
COMBLES	29th		Battalion and Transport had orders to be ready to move at 9 a.m., this order was cancelled at 11.30 with the possibility of moving in the afternoon but they received word they take prod. London Rye Dis'took over command Battalion from Major Pusson who	
	30th		to the proceeds to England on C.O.'s course	

W. Pheysey Jun?
Lt Col. 2nd R Munster Fus.

WAR DIARY or INTELLIGENCE SUMMARY

2nd Royal Munster Fusiliers — Army Form C. 2118 — OCTOBER 1918

Place	Date 1918	Hour	Summary of Events and Information	Remarks and references to Appendices
COMBLES.	1.Oct.		Paraded at 1200 hrs. and marched to NURLU, arriving 1830 hrs. delay caused owing to congestion of roads.	
NURLU.	2.Oct.		In the morning Coy Commanders reconnoitred road to EPEHY. Battalion paraded at 1415 hrs and marched to TETARD WOOD (EPEHY) which was reached at 1930 hrs. Some gas shelling during the night. Reconnoitring at	
BONY.	3rd Oct.		Received orders at 0200 hrs to march from EPEHY at 0330 hrs and take up position in trenches on N. side of GUILLEMONT FARM & Rde Reserve, and were in position at 0600 hrs. At 1200 hrs moved up into HINDENBURG LINE N. of BONY. The 151st Inf Bde who had attacked LE CATELET were driven back. At 1500 hrs "A" & "B" Coys took up position in CATELET line S. of village facing E. with left flank well thrown back at 1830 hrs Battn. was ordered to take up line S. of LE CATELET facing N. "A" Coy on right, "B" Coy on the centre, "C" in touch with 149 Inf Bde at MAQUINCOURT FARM, "D" Coy and HQ in Reserve in sunken road S. of LE CATELET. 2/Lt T.J. CARSON. wounded in arm by sniper. S.E. of LE CATELET.	150 Bde O.O. 192 A
LE CATELET	4 Oct.		At 0200 hrs The bndg. officer was called to Bde HQ. and received orders to attack LE CATELET and take LA PANNERIE SOUTH at 0610 hrs, in conjunction with 2nd Royal Irish Rifles on the left, with two Coys of the 2nd Northumberland Fusiliers to mop up. Runners were at once sent to Coy Commanders to attend Battn HQ, and for the Battn to assemble at the same time on "B" Coy, in the following order, first two waves "A" & "C", with a frontage of 450 yards each, 3rd wave to form 3rd wave, and "D" Coy with a frontage	150 Bde O.O. 193 B

2nd Royal Munster Fus.   1st Nov 1918   Army Form C. 2118.

WAR DIARY
or
INTELLIGENCE SUMMARY.
(Erase heading not required.)

Place	Date 1918	Hour	Summary of Events and Information	Remarks and references to Appendices
LE CATELET (cont.)	4th Oct		— a very difficult operation, well carried out, considering the ground had not been reconnoitred or seen by daylight. Faintly heavy shelling going on all the time. The battn. moved forward at 0600 hrs; in order to push up with the barrage, which commenced at 0610 hrs on a line three quarters of the way through the village. The battn. suffered very heavy casualties from machine gun nests in the village but managed to force its way through and gave the rising ground immediately to N. here "A" Coy lost direction and got on to lower slopes of PROSPECT HILL and did not gain such battn. until after the objective had been taken. "C" Coy came under very heavy T.M. and M.G. fire from their left, owing to the fact that the North Fus. had failed to keep up with the battn. 2/Lt K.V. FLANAGAN, although had received managed to lead his platoon close up to our objective. When he was wounded, a third time stuck to his post until nightfall when a sweep relieved. "D" Coy on Battn. Reserve, forced its way through the centre of the village through the gap left by "A" & "B" Coys until they were held up in N. end of village by two M.G. nests. Eventually these nests were ejected by the advance of our parties, attracted by the sound of the commanding officer's hunting horn, and the battn. was able to work up the CATELET to LE CATLET Rd without much opposition, and took their objective at 0915 hrs, which was consolidated and held, until 0200 hrs the following day. Our Coy who had lost touch was ordered at 2000 hrs to fill the gap between ourselves and the 7th WILTS Regt on the right. At nightfall this attack was organised to clear our left flank, i.e. ① in a Northerly direction from A in control ② in a Northerly direction from LE CATELET trench (by K.O.Y.L.I under orders O.C. 2/R Mun Fus.) ③ by "D" Coy in a South Westerly direction to enemy trenches in 5.29. This attack was not fully carried out and left flank made secure. The trenches hold by the battn. were heavily shelled in the afternoon, and Lieut CRISPIAN MC was killed.	Appendix

2nd Royal Munsters

WAR DIARY or INTELLIGENCE SUMMARY

Army Form C. 2118

October 1918

Place	Date 1918	Hour	Summary of Events and Information	Remarks and references to Appendices
LA PANNERIE SOUTH	5th Oct.		at 0200 rations arrived. At 0500, got orders for relief, and by 0630 were relieved by South Wales Bord. and went back to dugouts in railway embankment at GOUY. - slight shelling in morning. In afternoon "C" "D" occupied trenches in front of PROSPECT HILL, with "B" Coy in support. "B" Coy sent out parties to search for wounded - bring in dead - & salvage. About 12 o.r's got heavily shelled by H.E. "Mustard" gas, and several men sent to hospital owing to eyes being affected.	C
GOUY.	6th Oct.		About 0830 hrs, orders received to attack BEAUREVOIR LINE, 115th Inf Bde on our left, 7th Wills on right. "C" & "D" Coys formed first two waves. "A" Coy third wave, "B" Coy in reserve. One platoon of "D" Coy under Lieut E.D. CONRAN M.C occupied trenches in front of GUISENCOURT FARM. The battn. forced its way up to enemy wire, in spite of very heavy M.G. fire from prepared emplacements. Capt. T.O'BRIEN M.C. was killed trying to get through the wire, and Capt. V.D. O'MALLEY M.C. (H/Adjt) & Lieut A. KEEVIL M.B.E. M.C. Lt. E.B. RUSSELL were wounded. About 1730 hrs orders were received by the battn to be relieved by the 2nd R. Dublin Fus, and the battn. marched back to BONY, by Coys by 2230 hrs.	D
BONY.	7th Oct.		Cleaning up. The battn. under one hours notice to move	
BONY.	8th Oct.		Bde became host to the Reserve at 0500 hrs, & took its orders likewise to be prepared to move at short notice, which at 0915 hrs was changed to two hours notice. No shelling of the area after 0100 hrs. Transport moved to VENDHUILE	

2nd Royal Munsters

October 1918 — Army Form C. 2118.

WAR DIARY
or
INTELLIGENCE SUMMARY.
(Erase heading not required.)

Place	Date 1918	Hour	Summary of Events and Information	Remarks and references to Appendices
BONY.	9th Oct		Coys paraded at 0700 hrs and marched to GOUY & LECATELET to collect and bury dead at GOUY, where the Rev. Fr. R. MORRISEY C.F. arrived at 9 am. At 1130 hrs orders received to move at once. At 1345 hrs. battn marched through LE CATELET-GOUY-GUIZENCOURT FARM, where the Batn was inspected by the Divl Commander. Had tea at LE PETIT FOLIE FARM, & billeted for the night at SERAIN. Casualties. 1 O.R. NCOs - Lieut Dent Wounded. 5 O.R.s wounded.	150 ORs OR 196 F
REUMONT	10th Oct		Paraded at 0820 hrs and marched via LEPINNETTE to REUMONT, where batn was billeted for the night. Coy commanders reconnoitred roads to – LE CATEAU – ST. BENIN – ST. SOUPLET	G
REUMONT	11th Oct		Gas alarm between 0130 and 0200 hrs. At 1445 hrs Condg Officers conference at Bde Hdqrs. – 1530 hrs Condg Officer & Coy Cmdrs reconnoitre ST BENIN which we take over tonight. – 1900 – 2000 hrs, batn left billets in REUMONT to relieve 7th & 75th Batns in the line as laid down in O.O. 4 of this date. Relief complete at 0100. Casualties 1 O.R. killed T.L. & 1 tank wounded Battn HQ Q 19 central	
ST BENIN	12th Oct		At 0500 hrs heavy shelling along front line – 1400 Battle Surplus joined at Transport lines following officers sent to rejoin their Corps. 1/t PRENDERGAST to "D" Coy, 2/t W. WHATELY 1/t H.W. CLARKE to "B" (Capt. C.C. SMYTHE to Transport lines (on rest) Capt T.E. TOLLER Med. H.G. CATTLIN to "C" Lieut T.R. MOWE to "D". Casualties 5 other ranks wounded. 1 O.R. missing	
Coy Central ST BENIN	13th Oct		Capt. C.C. SMYTHE 2/t Lieut P.T. FARRELL to Transport lines. Lieut C.R. WILLIAMS T.C. took over command of the Batn. Lieut Col. MAC JONSON-RYE D.S.O. to Transport lines for rest	

2nd Royal Munster Fusiliers October 1918

WAR DIARY
or
INTELLIGENCE SUMMARY

Army Form C. 2118.

Place	Date	Hour	Summary of Events and Information	Remarks and references to Appendices
ST. BENIN (cont)	13/10/18		Casualties Lt. E.D. CONRAN M.C. wounded. Transport lines (BEVMONT) heavily shelled	
S.T. BENIN	14/10/18		Transport lines moved back to BERTRY at 0110 hrs.	
			At 0330 hrs Battn HQ hit by shell - moved into ditch at Q.19.a.8.2. - one L.G. & "A" Coy hut out of action by enemy shell - decrease of gas shelling - own section of line reconnoitred by 149 & 151 Inf. Bdes - Patrols reconnoitred crossings at River SELLE - all tried on & nowhere. Nos 13390 Cpl. S. Campbell & 7108 L/Cpl. S. Shaw G killed by shell after delivery of rations	1
ST. BENIN	15/10/18		At 0300 Cross Roads Q.19 central shelled (Gas M.E.) Battn Hdqrs again moved to ditch Q.19.D.a.8.2. All telephone wires & 5 bicycles destroyed during two shellings - remnants of "B" Coy ordered to re-inforce line held by 1st Welsh. "C" Coy ordered to re-inforce line held by 1st Welsh. 12 wounded Tetherly (gas). 1300hrs Cmdg Officers Conference with Bde Cmdr at Battn HQ re impending operations. "C" Coy ordered to re-inforce line held by 1st Welsh. New Battn HQ at Q.19.C.7.6 prepared, owing to harassing shellfire. Lieut M. PRENDERGAST wounded (on patrol)	
		2200 hrs	B'n H.Q. moved to Q.19.C.7.6	

2nd Royal Munster Fus.

WAR DIARY
or
INTELLIGENCE SUMMARY.
(Erase heading not required.)

Army Form C. 2118.

1918.

Instructions regarding War Diaries and Intelligence Summaries are contained in F.S. Regs., Part II. and the Staff Manual respectively. Title pages will be prepared in manuscript.

Place	Date	Hour	Summary of Events and Information	Remarks and references to Appendices
ST BENIN	16/10/18	0230-0330	Enemy shelled main road Q.19.C (near Bn H.Q.) & Farm Q.19 Central. 0600 hrs. Bn HQ. returned to Bn HQ.	
		0930	O.C. Bn at Conference Bde H.Q.	
		1000 hrs	Coy Comdrs. 2/R Dub. Fus. Sent round line with a view to relieving Bn.	K
		1400 hrs	Conference of Coy Comdrs at Bn. HQ.	
		1730	Guide met 2/R Dub. Fus. Coys. at Q.19 central (for day) & Railway arch Q.19.D (for ABC Coys)	
		2100	Relief by 2/R Dub Fus.	
		2115 hrs	Bn HQ. moved to Q.26.a.48.	00B
			Completed 4 gas cases to hospital from C. Coy.	
			Casualties	

"Trench" Strength of Batln.		Officers	O.R.
A Coy.		1	59
B		3	73
C		2	47
D		2	92
HQ.		4	45
		11	316

M.O. & H² 1
1/9 A.A. Leinster, Transport, Administration 1 9.5
13 411

A6945 Wt. W11422/M1160 35,000 12/16 D. D. & L. Forms/C2118/14.

2nd Royal Munster Fus.

October 1916.

Army Form C. 2118.

WAR DIARY
or
INTELLIGENCE SUMMARY.
(Erase heading not required.)

Instructions regarding War Diaries and Intelligence Summaries are contained in F. S. Regs., Part II. and the Staff Manual respectively. Title pages will be prepared in manuscript.

Place	Date	Hour	Summary of Events and Information	Remarks and references to Appendices
ST BENIN ST SOUPLET	17/10/18	0530	Barrage for attack across R. SELLE opened. 130 R.I. on right — very weak & practically no shelling by enemy. Batn. ordered to stand by.	
		0800	Actn. H.Q. C.O. R.I called for to attend conference at Actn. H.Q. (Q.19 cent).	
		0915	Bn. moved up in rear of 2/160 2nd Bn. across R. SELLE North of ST SOUPLET.	
		1100 hrs	Batn. dug in on two sides of railway embankment Q.22.R. in Trenches ⁷/wide on left and W.1928.C. on right	✓
		1415	C.O. at conference with Bn. H.Q. (Q.28.A) — 130 hrs. Break ¾/10	
		1700 hrs	Bn. placed under orders of Lt Col Mullen (?)	
			1/K.O.Y.L.I. C.O.+Adj. proceeded to see C.O. 1/K.O.Y.L.I. (Q.15.C.39)	
		2000 hrs	Bn. arrived at (Morin) H.Q. & drew hot rations.	
		2100	Bn. moved out to Q.15.B.0 on top of 21 post. "A" in support. "C" in reserve with "B+D" Coys frontline. 2 prisoners taken. Batn. H.Q. at Q.15.B.15.	
SLE CATEAU	18/10/18	0130	Orders for attack at 0530 received. Coy Cmdrs sent for.	
		0430	Objective etc explained to Coy Cmdrs.	

2nd R. Munster Regt.   October 1918.   Army Form C. 2118.

WAR DIARY
or
INTELLIGENCE SUMMARY.
(Erase heading not required.)

Place	Date	Hour	Summary of Events and Information	Remarks and references to Appendices
S. LE CATEAU (continued)	18/10/18	0530	Barrage for attack put down. 2/R.M.F. on right, 2/R.D.F. on left. 1/Royal. in support & all under command of Lt. Col. Matterson D.S.O.	
		0535	Very heavy hostile counter barrage put down inflicting many casualties in Bazuel by.	
		0730	Battn. seized objective & pushed on towards BAZUEL. Being too exhausted to carry the second bdy. of wire not emporarily fully established objections to men prior to attack. It was found that overhead fire in front of barrage put down for 25 min. & had to be withdrawn. Casualties — Lt. W.R. Howe and 25 O.R. killed. 2Lieut. D. Monahan Bur, H.W. Clarke, W.H.G. Carolan & 69 O.R. wounded. 14 O.R. missing.	M
			Battn. consolidated on line Q6d - Q12 cent - Q12c. Battn. very mixed up with 2/R.D.F. & 1/Royal. Battn. captured battery of 6 machine guns in Q.12 A.	

2nd R. Munster Fus.

October 1918.

Army Form C. 2118.

WAR DIARY
or
INTELLIGENCE SUMMARY.
(Erase heading not required.)

Place	Date	Hour	Summary of Events and Information	Remarks and references to Appendices
BAZUEL	19/10/18		During night 18/19 Batt. had a few casualties from minnenwerfer fire. Ottuma Quiet night & day. Batt. H.Q. in sunken road near Orchard J.27.C	
		1200 hrs	Batt. withdrawn from forward area (2.8.9.0) having moved Murphy's line) & moved to MARETZ in motor Lorries, proceeded with Bde.	
MARETZ	20/10/18		Congratulatory Messages of Divl. commander & others on parade. Nothing unusual. Occurred. except B. moved to be ready to relieve to REUMEN (U.6.b.6.6.) Terminus (U/19/D/9). Warning Order preparing for 24 hrs at 22.30 hrs	
MARETZ	21/10/18		Capt. C.R. Williams M.C. appointed Acting. O/Maj. B.H. Pardoe at Senior Officers School Aldershot. Men sent to Divisional Baths Cleaning morning. Lieut. T.O. Dodd rejoined from malaria details Dieppe. 2/Lt. Pegum, 2/Lt. Edgar, & 2/Lt. Guerin joined from Base.	
MARETZ	22/10/18		Morning wet. 2/Lt. Stone joined from Base & 2/Lt. Rogers rejoined from malaria. Reinforcement 41 O.R. from Base & proceeded to attached to Y/R Coy as joined	

2nd Royal Munster Fus.   October 1918.

Army Form C. 2118.

WAR DIARY
INTELLIGENCE SUMMARY.
(Erase heading not required.)

Place	Date	Hour	Summary of Events and Information	Remarks and references to Appendices
MARETZ	23/10/18	1800	Major Gen. JACKSON A.S.O. Comdg. 50' Div. presented immediate awards to 20079 Pte Slaven, 6188 Pte Murphy, 20643 Sgt H. Smith, 20302 Pte A. Stanley, 6253 Sgt W. Egan, 14111 Cpl. T. Lawlor, 1921 Pte P. Eaton all awarded military medals for conduct in LE CATELET actions 5-7 Oct. 1918. Also presented bars to D.C.M. earned by R.S.M. RINGWOOD earned in March 1918. Following were also awarded military medals for LE CATELET actions 3rd-7th Oct. but were not available 8633 Cpl W. Brickley (wounded), 5931 Gd W. Taylor (wounded-pow), 20320 L/C F. Docherty (killed 18/10/18), 5970 Pte P. Freeman, 2568 Gd J. Offerman (on escort duty at Base) 986 Sgt Hyde D.C.M. (wounded), 113 2/Lt T. Payne (missing 12/10/18), 8385 2/Lt J Bryant (wounded)	
MARETZ	24/10/18	1000	G.O.C. 150 Bde inspected transport of Battn. Coys at Training. Lieut Rathorne 2/Lieut Godsell & 2/Lt. Grant reported arrival from 1MM U.K. 2/Lt Clarke returned from leave e/o 13 O.R. returned from hospital.	
MARETZ	25/10/18		Coys at training in morning.	
MARETZ	26/10/18		Draft 136 O.R. joined from Base & Inlandria details Marten Eglise 23 O.R. Base draft consisted of 13 O.R. from 2/R.M.F. 4 " " 3/East Yorks 22 O.R. from 3/K.R.F. Border Regt.	

2nd Royal Munster Fus. WAR DIARY October 1918

Place	Date	Hour	Summary of Events and Information	Remarks
MARETZ	27/10/18		Sunday. Church parades & rest.	
MARETZ	28/10/18		Coys. at training in morning. 140 O.R. received orders to be ready to move at 10 o'hrs. tomorrow.	M
MARETZ	29/10/18	08.45	Bn paraded & marched out of Maretz passing starting point 10 o'hrs & proceeded to LE CATEAU via Busigny. Bn billeted in RUE de LANDRECIES. C.O. went up to 5th Bde area via G.O.T. 150	
LE CATEAU			Role to reconnoitre area to be taken over tomorrow. Following awarded M.M. for conduct on 18/10/18. 20260 Cpl. W.P. Trew. 811 Pte D. Williams. 5265 Pte M. M°Carthy 9112 C.S.M. S. Tyrrell. 202 CSM P. Fergus. Arial bn to medal awarded to 25768 Cpl. J. O'Gorman. M.M.	
LE CATEAU	30/10/18	07.00	Strong enemy shower of bombing enemy plane. A few H.E. shells fell in vicinity of HQrs. Coy. left Cajnjis Sgt. 1st gave Sgt Bordes sph proceeded to Bordes to reconnoitre line. 13.45 Bn paraded & marched to Bn Billets. Bn Hd. Staff re-remained in LE CATEAU.	

2nd Royal Munster Fus.
October 1918

WAR DIARY
or
INTELLIGENCE SUMMARY

Army Form C. 2118.

Place	Date	Hour	Summary of Events and Information	Remarks and references to Appendices
ROBERSART	20/10/18		Battalion took over the line from the 2nd Bedfords, relief complete at 5.55. There was a certain amount of shelling (enemy's) on H.Q. also some directed on to fires to the road in front of Bn H.Q. A & B Coys were in the line and C Coy in Reserve.	
ROBERSART	21.10.18		C & H.Q. shelling caused casualties. H.Q. moved and signaled to evacuate house of Bridaught and 6 a.m. The day passed quietly. Battn were relieved by 1st 1st and marched back to LE CATEAU. Capt Snyffer was wounded on the 1st by whole machine gun fire when marching into BASSE	

Murnane Major
2nd Bn R. Munster Fusiliers.

SECRET.
Copy No. 3

150TH INFANTRY BRIGADE OPERATION ORDER NO. 192

Ref. Map MONTEBREHAIN 1/20,000   3rd October, 1918.

1. 2nd Australian Division will attack tomorrow at Zero hour, and will capture the GREEN LINE as shewn on attached map* and exploit to the RED LINE, forming their own defensive flank along the MASNIERES - BEAUREVOIR Line.
   * Marked on Liaison Officers Maps.

2. 50th Division will co-operate as follows :-
   Artillery. (a) Keep high ground in squares S.25 and 26 and area GOUY - RUE NEUVE under fire.

   Infantry. (b) The 151st Inf.Bde. and Right Battalion of 149th Inf.Bde. are to press forward patrols through GOUY and LE CATELET followed by formed bodies.

   The Dividing line between 149th and 151st Infantry Brigades will be VAUBAN VALLEY - QUINCAMPAIX Mill - A.4 central; between 151st Inf.Bde. and 2nd Australian Division a line drawn from A.18 central to T.26 central.

3. The 2nd Bn. North'd Fusiliers will move to A.15 central at 0300 hrs. 3rd instant and will come under orders of G.O.C. 151st Infantry Brigade. Orders have been issued separately.

4. The 150th Infantry Brigade less 2nd Bn. North'd Fusiliers and 150th L.T.M. Battery will take up a position in the GUILLEMONT FARM trench system. Trenches North of the GUILLEMONT ROAD are allotted to the 2nd Bn. R.Munster Fusiliers, trenches South of the Road to the 7th Bn. Wiltshire Regt.
   Brigade Headquarters in DUNCAN'S POST.
   March will be carried out as follows :-

   Starting Point CURD COPSE (F.15.a.)
   7th Bn. Wiltshire Regt. will pass S.P. at 0400 hrs.) Route
   2nd Bn. R.Munster Fusiliers at 0425 hrs.   ) GUILLEMONT
   150th Inf.Bde. Hd.Qrs. at 0450 hrs.   ) ROAD.

   Usual intervals plus 50 yds. between platoons.
   Dress - Fighting Order.

5. Officers Commanding Battalions will take forward such transport as they require; this will return to ENEMY lines when loads are dumped and will be Brigaded and moved forward under Brigade arrangements.

6. Separate instructions are being issued re rations and surplus kits.

7. Brigade Hd.Qrs. will close in present position at 0430 hrs. and will open at DUNCAN'S POST F.17.d. at the same hour.

8. Battalions will send their liaison Officer and 2 runners to Brigade Hd.Qrs. when the assembly is completed.

9. 150th L.T.M. Battery will not move until further orders.

10. Watches of liaison Officers have been synchronised.

11. Prisoners to TOMBOIS FARM.
    ACKNOWLEDGE.

Issued at 0100 hrs.   Captain, Brigade Major,
Through Signals.   150th Infantry Brigade.

Distribution
overleaf.

Copy No. 1. 2nd Bn. North'd Fus.
"   " 2. 7th Bn. Wiltshire Regt.
"   " 3. 2nd Bn. R.Munster Fusiliers.
"   " 4. 150th L.T.M.Battery.
"   " 5. 149th Infantry Brigade.
"   " 6. 151st Infantry Brigade.
"   " 7. 50th Division.
"   " 8. File.
"   " 9. War Diary.

Operation Order No 192.

① 2nd Australian Division orders:—
2nd Australian Div has ordered following line to be reached tonight AAA. B.30.a - B.29 central - B.22 central - B.15 central - B.8 central. Ends.

② 20th Bn. Manchester Regt may relieve portion of 2nd Australian Div tonight.

③ 1st Bn. K.O.Y.L.I. have obtained touch with Australians at B.2.c.7.4.

④ ~~sos barrage lines for~~

B.

Order No 7. 2/R Munster Fus

Ref Map
MONTBREHAIN.   4/10/18

① The 150 Inf Bde will attack at 0610
4th inst. and will capture the high ground
N. of LE CATELET.

② 2 R Munster Fusrs. will attack on the
right — 3rd Royal Fusrs on the left.
The battn. will be formed up on a line
through LE CATELET & GOUY, which
are marked on map.

 — A Coy. on the right B Coy. on the
left. C Coy. in Support D Coy in Reserve

Division between Coys a line through
corner of LE CATELET TRENCH - A.11.a.7.7
Road junction - A.5.6.2.4. R of Rd LA
PANNERIE.
Objectives + dividing lines have been marked
on Coy. Comdrs maps

B

Normal "Tactics" will follow behind
tatts and mop up LE CATELET and
GOUY.

Reserve Coys will mop up final objectives

Barrage will commence on barrage
line at 0b10 & will continue there for
6 minutes, and will subsequently advance
at rate of 100 yds per 4 minutes
Reports to Reserve Coy every half hour

ACKNOWLEDGE.

(Sd) V.D. O'Malley
Capt: M.Adjt.

4/10/18   2 & Munster Fuslrs

150th Brigade.

Captured LA PANNERIE
SOUTH 21-09-45. There
was a great deal of resistance
in LE CATELET When the
Right of Company was held up
this morning. Received by Rochwell, who
"Can you send any help as
I can only find less than
100 men." I have not been
able to get in with the Left
Batt. but some of the Battn about
2/0 strong are in LE CATELET
trenches.

16-20   Thompson Lt Col
                              R.W.F
4-10-18

150 M Bde [B] T.R.1

We have been forced to retire about 150 yds from LA PANNERIE SOUTH owing to our left flank being entirely exposed and scarcity of men but have now got patrols on the road immediately W of LA PANNERIE. We have not yet got contact with left Battalion. Estimated casualties 10 O/R, 150 ORs

Present position =
Trench S.29.b.0.3 to S.29.b.7.0 and trench running Southwards from h of LA PANNERIE SOUTH

H.Qrs at Southern junction of these trenches. We are in touch with

All avail. W.L. Carriers to
the East of the road at
RUE NEUVE.
All available
Stretchers will be taken
by this party.

O/C A Coy will detail
2 men to accompany
B Coys mopping up
party to show the ground
over which their Coy
advanced.

~~Reinforcements to be~~ sent out at 1400.

H Mullen
Capt (R)
2 Kents

1130
5/10/18

Whistler
Toller fireplace News
Carolus C
Howe D
O'Farrel C, M.
Boing D
Davenport A
Curran B

To O.C. "B" Coy.   A.D.2

O.C. "B" will detail the
following parties:-

1 NCO & 10 men as
Salvage party to collect
salvage east of the ground
over which the advance
to LE CATELET was
made. A salvage dump
will be established on
road just S of QUINCANPRIX
mill.

Remainder of Coy to
be organised into parties
to mop up and clear
western portion of LE CATELET
over ground of the advance,
and to search for wounded
and collect dead.

occupied by us.

Coys to be in position by 1pm posts in front. Bn HQrs where was.

Bn HQrs as at present.

D Coy will establish a strong point at ~~for~~ trench junction at S.30.d. 6.5.

ACKNOWLEDGE

J. M[...]
Capt & Adjt
[...]

1110
5/10

O/C H.D.C.D. No. C

The following re-organiz-
ation in front will take place
to-day.

The Batt'n will take
over the left sector of
Bde front as follows:-

D Coy from S 30 c 3.4
to road junction with bench
at S 30 d 6.9.

C Coy from road junction
at S 30 d 6.4 (inclusive)
to T 25 c 6 2.

A Coy in support in
Sunken road about A 6 d. 5.1

B Coy in reserve @ in
dug-out lines presently

Tks Wks in LE CATELET
NAUROY LINE S.29.a.90.
Shneider stop herewith
We should have 110 troops
SAA & 10 boxes Mills
grenades

12.35   Thours ?

4/10/18   Lt Col cdg
                         2 Rnewst Frs

Prefix......Code......m.			Date......
Office of Origin and Service Instructions	Sent	Service.	From......
S.13 PRIORITY	At ......m. To ...... By	(Signature of "Franking Officer")	By......

TO		NUWI	

Sender's Number.	Day of Month.	In reply to Number.	AAA
C3	5		

115 Inf Bde are advancing today from S.28 and S.29 in a NORTH easterly direction and expect to reach line AUBENCHEUL-AUX-BOIS cross roads T.20.C. inclusive. 15 150 Inf Bde aaa ROME will send out a company to cover right flank of their advance aaa dividing line between brigades on final objective east line T.20.D.0.0 aaa company will advance by bounds moving off when troops of 115 B extent trench section T.30.B. aaa first bound VAUXHALL QUARRY second bound line from cross roads T.20.20.C

From: cross roads T.20.20.C
Place: T.26.D.0.0 aaa
Time:

The above may be forwarded as now corrected. (Z)

Censor. Signature of Addressor or person authorised to telegraph in his name
* This line should be erased if not required.

"A" Form
MESSAGES AND SIGNALS.

Army Form C. 2121
(In pads of 100.)

garrison will be left in
VAUXHALL QUARRY aaa strong points
will be established at own trench
T.1.B. and at BEAUREVOIR LINE at
T.20.a.0 central and T.26.a.5.5
also about T.26.D.4.0 about
already made aaa garrison
will patrol to each flank
and obtain touch especially
with 11 Surfolks on left and
25 Div. at 96 UZ.18 COURT
FARM T.26.0 aaa company
will mop up small parties
but will not attempt
overcome strong opposition
NUW1 will be prepared to
place one company at

"A" Form
MESSAGES AND SIGNALS.

Army Form C. 2121
(In pads of 100.)

Office of Origin and Service Instructions: **SR Proovly**

From: **R.O.3 Cope**

TO: **NUW1**

Sender's Number: **C3**

disposal of ROME aaa until line firmly established & present line will be held aaa 115 INF BDE will move shortly ACKNOWLEDGE

From / Place / Time: **150 y. B.** **1210**

"A" Form
MESSAGES AND SIGNALS.

Army Form C. 2121
(In pads of 100.)

Sender's Number.	Day of Month.	In reply to Number.	AAA
E6	5		

The Bde will not be relieved tonight aaa Situation is 115 Bde hold AUBENCHEUL-AUX-BOIS with right about T.19 central aaa situation on right is obscure 25th Div do not hold BEAUREVOIR on South & COURT FME aaa Dispositions of 150/B on night 5/6 will be S.24.C.1.9 to BANTEUX IE South inclusive one Coy 2nd NF aaa S.29.D.9.5 to S.30.D.8.4

"A" Form
MESSAGES AND SIGNALS.

Army Form C. 2121
(In pads of 100.)

2 Coy 2 RNF aaa
S30D8.4 to B2A0.5 one
Coy 2 NF one Coy 4 Wilts
aaa B2A0.5 to B2 Central
one Coy 4 Wilts aaa One
Reserve Coy 4 Wilts with
left on SUNKEN ROAD
running N & S through
B.1.C aaa 1 Reserve Coy
2nd RNF with right
on this SUNKEN ROAD
aaa 1 Reserve Coy 2 RNF
on S of LE CATELET
aaa 2 Reserve Coy 2 NF
on N of LE CATELET aaa
1 Coy 4 Wilts will have
1 Coy in T19D & T25B

"A" Form
MESSAGES AND SIGNALS.

Army Form C. 2121
(In pads of 100.)

Picketing the roads & keeping touch with main line. 2 Rifle & 115 bn coy Horse in VAUXHALL OSSPRY aaa 2 NF will place 1 coy at disposal of 4 Wilts aaa 4 Wilts will send Officers patrols to ascertain position at GOUZINCOURT FME 1st patrol to go out at once 2nd about 0100 hrs & a just before dawn report will be forwarded after each patrol aaa above dispositions will be taken up at once 4 Wilts

"A" Form
MESSAGES AND SIGNALS.

Army Form C. 2121 (In pads of 100.)

will make every endeavour to get touch on right

acknowledge

From: 150
Place: 13
Time: 1945

"A" Form
MESSAGES AND SIGNALS.

Army Form C. 2121
(In pads of 100)

Prefix......... Code...........m	Words. Charge.	This message is on a/c of:	Recd. at...........m
(Office of Origin and Service Instructions)	Sent		Date..............
....	At...............m	.... Service.	From.............
....	To...............		
	By..............	(Signature of "Franking Officer.")	By...............

TO:
- 2. N.F. ~~115~~ Bde.
- 7. Wilts ~~50~~ ~~Bn~~
- 2. R.M.F.

Sender's Number.	Day of Month.	In reply to Number.	AAA
* C.9.	6.		

Situation	reported	BEAUREVOIR	in
our	hands	GOUZINCOURT	FME
~~is~~ NOT	in	our	possession
right	of	115	Bde.
about	S 24	central	AAA
7th	150	1/4	Bde
will move	get	into	position
to	attack	BEAUREVOIR	LINE
AAA	Lt Col	TONSON	RYE will
~~	~~up~~	form	up
on	line	T. 19. central	to
our	line	South	T. 25. central
AAA	Troops	will	be
~~formed~~	up	in	depth
North'd	Fusiliers	on	left
Munster	Fusiliers	on	right. AAA
2nd	Bn	North'd	~~~~

From...........
Place...........
Time............

The above may be forwarded as now corrected. (Z)

....
Censor.   Signature of Addressee or person authorised to telegraph in his name.

* This line should be erased if not required.

"A" Form
MESSAGES AND SIGNALS.

Army Form C. 2121
(In pads of 100)

No. of Message..............

Prefix......... Code..........	Words.	Charge.	This message is on a/c of:	Recd. at.........m.
Office of Origin and Service Instructions	Sent			Date...........
....	At............m.		.... Service.	From ....
....	To..............			
....	By..............		(Signature of "Franking Officer.")	By ....

| TO | | 2 | | |

Sender's Number.	Day of Month.	In reply to Number.	AAA
* G 9			

will	come	under	order
Col.	TONSON	RYE	AAA
attack	will	not	take
place	until	further	orders
but	patrol	will	push
forward	to	BEAUREVOIR	line
AAA	7th	WILTS.	will
attack	GOUZINCOURT	FME	with
2	companies	from	the
West	and	South	west
as	soon	as	the
Batt'n	Commdr	is	ready
AAA	there	will	be
no organized	artillery	preparation	but
O.C.	will	will	arrange
for	our	barrage	as
required	will	O.C.	Machine

From
Place
Time

The above may be forwarded as now corrected. (Z)

....

Censor. Signature of Addresser or person authorised to telegraph in his name.

* This line should be erased if not required.

"A" Form
MESSAGES AND SIGNALS.

Army Form C. 2121
(In pads of 100)

No. of Message..............

Prefix......... Code.........m	Words. Charge.	This message is on a/c of:	Recd. at.........m.
Office of Origin and Service Instructions	Sent	..................Service.	Date...............
....	At............m.		From.............
.... To........		(Signature of "Franking Officer.")	By...............
.... By........			

TO		3		
	Sender's Number.	Day of Month.	In reply to Number.	AAA
*	C.9			

guns	AAA	remaining	two
companies	Wills	will	hold
old	line	on	N.E. of
PROSPECT	HILL	AAA	Pargord
HQs	will	close	at
present	position	at	09.15 hrs
and	will	open	same
hour	at	2nd	B.
MUNSTER	Two	Headquarters	A.11.d.5.5.
when	all	reports	will
be	sent	AAA	Batt.
comdn	must	report	location
of	their	Headquarters	
ACKNOWLEDGE			

From	150	M Bde	May
Place			
Time	0805		

The above may be forwarded as now corrected. (Z)

.... Censor.   Signature of Addressor or person authorised to telegraph in his name.

* This line should be erased if not required.

SECRET

Brigade Operation Order No 184

Ref: 57 c NE 1/20000

1. 50th Division in co-operation with 66th Div on Left & 27 American Div on Right will continue advance tomorrow to RED LINE (today's objection for 149 Inf Bde)

2. Lt Col MALLINSON'S GROUP will attack on a 3 Battalion front with 2nd Lancaster Fus and 8th R Scots Fus in line, and remnants of 1st KOYLI in support.
Front. R.7.c.8.6. to Q.6.d.7.5.
Right Boundary - Q.17.c.9.5 to R.7.c.8.6
Left Boundary - Q.10.d.8.8 to Q.6.d.7.5

3. 7th Bn Wilts will attack on Right & Scottish Horse on Left of Lt Col MALLINSON'S Group.

4. Barrage will come down at ZERO 200 Yards East of DOTTED RED LINE Where it will remain for 3 minutes, thence advancing at rate of 100 Yards every 3 minutes.

5. Two hours after capture of RED LINE a Brigade of 25th Division will pass through & capture todays BROWN LINE

6. Closest liaison will be maintained with both flanks

7. Every man of leading Infantry will

2

light "Ground flares" when called for
by "Contact" Planes

8. Zero hour will be 05:20 hours

9. Brigade HQ will remain at
Q.19 central.

10. Acknowledge.

L. Long, Captain
for 13th Inf Bde.

Issued at 8.45 p.m. To all Concerned.

F

SECRET.

Copy No. 6

150TH INFANTRY BRIGADE OPERATION ORDER NO. 196.

Reference Map 57 1/40,000 10th October 1918

1. The 150th Infantry Brigade will march to REUMONT on the 10th October 1918 in accordance with march table attached.

Troop Northd
   Hussars.
7th Bn.
  Wilts Regt.
1 Sec. "D" Coy
50th Bn. M.G.
   Corps.

2. An Advance Guard under command of Lieut. Colonel H.J. HODGSON, 7th Bn. Wiltshire Regt., composed as per margin, will precede the main body by 500 yards.

3. The 150th Infantry Brigade Group will be composed of :-
   2nd Bn. North'd Fusiliers.
   7th Bn. Wiltshire Regt.
   2nd Bn. R. Munster Fusiliers.
   150th Trench Mortar Battery.
   "D" Coy., 50th Bn. M.G. Corps.
   TROOP North'd Hussars.
   Detachment XIII Corps Cyclists Battn.
   No. 3 Coy., Train.
   ~~Field Coy., R.E.~~
   ~~Field Ambulance.~~

4. Transport will march as follows :-
   Lewis gun limbers and pack mules in rear of companies.
   "A" Echelon less above in rear of Battalions.
   "B" Echelon Transport in rear of column in order of march of units.

5. Separate orders will be issued about supplies.

6. Separate orders will be issued for Field Ambulance.

7. Brigade Headquarters will march at head of main body. Officers Commanding Battalions and O.C. "D" Coy, 50th Bn. M.G. Corps will march with Brigade Headquarters.

8. Acknowledge.

Issued at 0515 hrs.
thro' Signals.

Captain,
Brigade Major,
150th Infantry Bde.

Copy No. 1. G.O.C.
2. Staff Captain.
3. S.S.O.
4. 2nd Bn. North'd Fusiliers.
5. 7th Bn. Wiltshire Regt.
6. 2nd Bn. R. Munster Fus.
7. 150th L, Trench Mortar Bty.
8. "D" Coy., 50th Bn. M.G.C.
9. O.C. Troop, North'd Hussars.
10. O.C. Det'ment XIII Corps Cyclist Battn.
11. 50th Divn.
12. No. 3 Coy, Train.
13. ~~Field Coy, R.E.~~
14. ~~Field Ambce.~~
15. War Diary.
16. File.
17. File.

Rcd 0600 hrs.

MARCH TABLE TO ACCOMPANY OPERATION ORDER No. 196.

Serial No.	Unit.	Starting point.	Time.	Route.	Destination.
A.	Advance Guard.	Advance Guard marches under orders Advance Guard commander.			
B.	Bde. H.Q. & Signal Sec. Det. XIII Corps Cyclists Battn.	Junction of track and ELINCOURT - SERAIN road about U.14.b.5.2.	0845 hrs	By track cleared today from about U.14.b.5.2. - U.9.d. - direct to LEPINETTE cross roads P.25.d.	REUMONT.
C.	2nd Bn. R. Munster Fus.		0846 hrs		
D.	"D" Coy., 50th Bn. M.G. Corps (less 1 section).		0913 hrs		
E.	2nd Bn. North'd Fusiliers.		0918 hrs.		
F.	150th L. Trench Mortar Battery.		0935 hrs		
G.	"B" Echelon Transport.		0936 hrs		

SECRET.

G

Copy No. 6

150TH INFANTRY BRIGADE OPERATION ORDER No. 197.

11th October, 1918.

Reference Map - Sheet 57b 1/40,000.

1. **INTENTION.** The 150th Infantry Brigade will relieve the 25th Division and the Right Brigade of the 66th Division on night 11th/12th October, 1918.

2. **DISTRIBUTION.**
    (a) The 2nd Bn. R. Munster Fusiliers will take over the front held by the 74th and 75th Infantry Brigades, 25th Division, from FORK ROAD (Q.22.c.3.4.) along West bank of R. SELLE to road bridge over the R. SELLE in Q.9.b. Companies will be disposed approximately as follows :-
    1 company Q.22.c.3.4. to Q.21.b.6.6.
    1 company Q.21.b.6.6. to railway and road junction Q.15.b.5.1.
    1 company from Q.15.b.5.1. to Q.9.c.8.3. with post on road Bridge
    1 company about Q.20. in reserve   Q.9.b.
    Arrangements will be made mutually between G.O.C's 74th and 75th Infantry Brigades and O.C. 2nd Bn. R. Munster Fusiliers.

    (b) The 2nd Bn. North'd Fusiliers will take over a 1 company front from 199th Infantry Brigade on the West of LE CATEAU from road junction K.34.a.6.1. Southwards. Exact details will be arranged between G.O.C. 199th Infantry Brigade and O.C. 2nd Bn. North'd Fusiliers.
    1 company will hold front line system, 1 company in close support and 2 companies in valley running South-West from PONT DES 4 VAUX K.33.a.

    (c) 7th Bn. Wiltshire Regt. less 1 platoon will be in Brigade reserve in sunken road Q.19.a. and in work at Q.20.a.

    (d) The gap between left of 2nd Bn. R. Munster Fusiliers and right of 2nd Bn. North'd Fusiliers will be held by machine guns of 50th Bn. Machine Gun Corps. The O.C. 7th Bn. Wiltshire Regt. will place one platoon in bank Q.8.b. to maintain liaison between 2nd Bn. R. Munster Fusiliers and machine gun line.

3. Battalions will patrol their front vigorously to obtain information as to enemies position and strength, also state of roads, bridges, obstacles, wire, depth and width of R. SELLE.
    Patrols will not engage themselves in attack.
    The 2nd Bn. North'd Fusiliers will push strong patrols through LE CATEAU and into square Q.4.
    The 2nd Bn. R. Munster Fusiliers will patrol Eastwards from their front and into square Q.10.
    The enemy are reported to be holding the line of the railway through Q.21 central - Q.10 central - Q.35 central, also the factory at Q.4.c.6.3. Enemy patrols are reported in LE CATEAU.
    Information obtained will be forwarded to Brigade Headquarters as soon as possible.

4. **LIAISON.** It is of the utmost importance that the 2nd Bn. R. Munster Fusiliers maintains liaison with the American Corps on the right. The present point of touch is Q.22.c.3.4. It is not known if the Americans hold ST. SOUPLET.
    The 2nd Bn. North'd Fusiliers will maintain liaison on their left with the 198th Infantry Brigade (66th Division). Battalions will maintain liaison between themselves by patrols.
    3 Cyclists will be detailed to the 2nd Bn. North'd Fusiliers.

PTO

- (2) -

5. **MACHINE GUNS.** 1 Section "D" Coy., 50th Bn. M.G. Corps is allotted to 2nd Bn. R. Munster Fusiliers and 1 Section to 2nd Bn. North'd Fusiliers. Remaining Sections take up position on high ground S.W. of LE CATEAU to cover gap between 2nd Bn. North'd Fusiliers and 2nd Bn. R. Munster Fusiliers.

6. **TRANSPORT.** Transport lines will not move.

7. **BRIGADE HEADQUARTERS.** Brigade Headquarters will be established at P.29.d.3.1. The Staff Captain will remain at Brigade Headquarters in REUMONT. Messages may be handed in there.

8. **REPORTING OF RELIEF.** Relief completed will be reported by runner. Position of Battalion Headquarters and dispositions will be reported as soon as possible.

Acknowledge.

J.A. Dyson ????

Issued at 17.10 hrs
thro' Signals.

Captain,
Brigade Major,
150th Infantry Brigade.

```
Copy No.  1.  G.O.C.
          2.  Staff Captain.
          3.  B.S.O.
          4.  2nd Bn. North'd Fusiliers.
          5.  7th Bn. Wiltshire Regt.
          6.  2nd Bn. R. Munster Fusiliers.
          7.  150th L. Trench Mortar Battery.
          8.  "D" Coy., 50th Bn. M.G. Corps.
          9.  50th Division.
         10.  74th Infantry Brigade.
         11.  75th Infantry Brigade.
         12.  199th Infantry Brigade.
         13.  1/3rd North'd Field Ambulance (MAROIS)
         14.  War Diary.
         15.  File.
         16.  File.
```

SECRET. Copy No. _
B.M. 760
16-10-18

150th Infantry Brigade.
Instructions Forthcoming Operations No. 1.

16th October 1918.

Ref. Map attached.

1. The 50th Division in conjunction with 66th Division on the left and 27th American Division on the right is to carry out an attack on a date which will be notified later.

2. Boundaries objectives and forming up places are shewn on the attached map.

3. On the night 16/17th Oct. the 2nd Bn. Royal Munster Fus. will be relieved by a Battn. of the 149th Inf. Bde. and the 7th Bn. Wiltshire Regt. will be relieved by a Battn. of the 151st Inf. Bde. These Battns. will then come into reserve in positions shewn on attached map. G.O.C. 150th Inf. Bde will retain command of the front until ZERO hour.

4. H.Q's 149th and 151st Inf. Bdes will be established in house Q.19 central at 2359 hrs 16th inst. H.Q's 150th Inf. Bde. will move to house Q.19 central at ZERO hour. House will be vacated by H.Q's 2nd Bn. North'd Fus. and 2nd Bn. R. Munster Fus. by 2300 hours 16th inst.

5. 149th Inf. Bde. and 151st Inf. Bde. will be formed up as shewn on attached map by ZERO minus 4 hours.

At ZERO 151st Inf. Bde will advance under a barrage and capture the RED DOTTED LINE. After a pause the 149th Inf. Bde. will continue the advance and capture the RED LINE. If the Americans come up on the right the 150th Inf. Bde. with the 7th Bn. Wiltshire Regt. on the right and 2nd Bn. North'd Fus. on the left will attack through the 149th Inf. Bde. and capture the 2nd objective.

The 2nd Bn. R. Munster Fus. will be in reserve.

- 2 -

6. Preliminary moves of the 150th Inf. Bde will be:-

Bde will move at Z+3 hrs to Valley Q.18 central.

If the RED DOTTED LINE is captured the Brigade will move at about ZERO plus 2 hours to about Valley. Q.22.d - Q.29.a. If the RED LINE is captured the Brigade will move to valley in Q.18.a. and Q.12.c. under orders from Brigade.

7. Objectives will be consolidated in depth of 2nd objective by 150th Inf. Bde - 1st objective by 149th Inf. Bde - RED DOTTED LINE by 151st Inf. Bde.

8. Battalions will arrange to have all deficiencies of battle equipment, i.e. flares, spades, etc, also cookers waiting at their reserve positions on night 16/17th inst to meet them on relief.

9. ACKNOWLEDGE.

J.N. Dyson
Captain,
Brigade Major
150th Inf. Bde.

Copy No. 1. 2nd Bn. North'd Fus.
2. 7th Bn. Wiltshire Regt.
3. 2nd Bn. R. Munster Fus.
4. 150th Trench Mortar Bty.

150th Infantry Brigade
Instructions No 2

SECRET
Copy No 3

Ref Map 57B 1/40,000
(objective map issued to Commanding Officers)

BM 750/2
16.10.18

1. Para 5 Instructions No 1 is cancelled and following substituted:-

    AT ZERO 151st Inf. Bde. will cross the River SELLE in Q 28 A+C. Battn. will open out on the line of the Railway & attack the RED DOTTED LINE. The left Battn. moving N. astride the Railway.

    The leading Battn. 149th Inf. Bde. will cross the stream in rear of the 151st Inf. Bde. & will follow closely the left Battn 151st Inf. Bde. Leading Battn 149 Inf. Bde. will reform about Q 10. D. 0.0. Second Battn 149th Inf. Bde. will assemble about Q 29. A 5.9. Third Battn. will assemble about Q 16. D. 3.3.

    At ZERO plus 132, the 149th Inf. Bde. will advance through the 151st Inf. Bde. & will capture the RED LINE.

    At ZERO plus 3 hours the 150th Inf. Brigade will advance to valley Q 11. D - Q 18. D. 7th Bn Wiltshire Regt followed by the 2nd Bn. R. Munster Fusiliers will move by bridges in Q 28 A+C to about Q 18. D. 5.5. and Q 18. C.C. 5.5. respectively.

    2nd Bn. Northd. Fus. will move by bridge and ford at ST BENIN to about Q 12. C. 0.4.

2. If the Americans come up on the flank the 150th Inf. Bde. will be prepared to capture the second objective on receipt of orders from the G.O.C. 150th Inf. Bde.

    The attack will be carried out by the 7th Bn Wiltshire Regt on the right & the 2nd Bn Northd. Fus. on the left.

1

-2-

Inter Battn boundaries are shown on map issued to Bn Commanders. After the capture of the final objective the 7th Bn Welsh Regt will be responsible for consolidating the front from the Right Divisional boundary to the BASUEL-POMMEREUIL Road inclusive.

The 2nd Bn R Munster Fus will be in support. O.C. 2nd Bn R Munster Fus will detail 2 companies to mop up BASUEL. These companies will be allotted definite objectives. The other two companies will remain in the hands of the Battn. Commander to be used for counter attack purposes or to assist either of the leading Battns.

3. R.A.F. contact planes will:-

(a) (i) Call for flares on the 2nd objective at ZERO plus 7 hours.

(ii) Ditto at ZERO plus 8 hours.

(iii) Ditto just before dusk.

4 men per platoon of leading infantry will light their flares each time the contact plane calls, remainder of men will wear their helmet pieces of paper etc.

O.s. C. Bns will impress on all ranks the importance of carrying out this order.

(b) A counter attack plane will be up all day. This machine will drop white parachute lights immediately over the counter attacking infantry.

4. The Nthb. Bn. North'd Fus. will establish a joint liaison post with 149th Inf. Bde. & 66th Divn. at R.36.D.4.8.

7th Bn. Welch Regt. will establish a joint liaison post with 27th American Divn. at house R.10.A.2.6. and on road R.9.C.0.5.

2nd Bn. R. Munster Fus. will establish joint posts with 27th American Divn. at road R.14.B.0.6.

5. Advance Bde. Hqrs. will be established at Farm Q.19 central at 2000 hrs. 16th inst. It will move in rear of leading Bns. to vicinity of LE QUENNELET GRANGE.

When the 150th Inf. Bde. advances, Advanced Bde. Headquarters will be established in vicinity of track in R.7.C.

All messages for Brigade Hqrs. will be sent VIA Advanced Brigade Headquarters. Communication between Advanced Brigade Headquarters & Battns. will be by means of lamp & runner & in the case of the Right Battn. by wireless.

Whenever a Battn. Headquarters is established two runners will be sent to Advanced Bde. Hqrs. When these men report a similar number will be returned to the Battn.

6. 150th Inf. Bde. Hqrs. will be in present position at ZERO. At ZERO plus 40 Headquarters will move to Farm Q.19 central & at ZERO plus 6 hours will move to LE QUENNELET GRANGE Q.24.A.

7. ACKNOWLEDGE

Issued at
Itno' Tyonh

Headquarters
150th Inf. Bde.
16 Octr. 1918.

Captain
Bde. Major
150 Inf. Bde.

Copy No 1. 2nd Bn North Fus
2. 7 Welsh Regt.
3. 2nd Bn R. Munn Fus
4. 156 T.M Batty
5. 50 Divn
6. 50th Bn L.G.C
7. 76. Bde R.F.A
8. 112 Bde R.F.A
9. 5th American Bde
10. S.C.
11. B.S.O.
12. File

(1086) Wt.W16552/M1615 250,000 Pads. 21/3/17. J.R.&C. E 685 Forms/C2122/6.

Army Form C2122
"B" Form. (In pads of 150)
MESSAGES AND SIGNALS. No. of Message..........

Prefix......Code......m.		Received	Sent	Office Stamp
Office of Origin and Service Instructions.	Words	At.........m.	At.........m.	*Secret.*
		From..........	To..........	
		By..........	By..........	

TO: GOT.A. / ROME TOWN. R.F.C. / NUW1.

Sender's Number	Day of Month	In reply to Number	AAA
BX.31	16	—	

The order for the advance from the RED LINE will be sent to Battn Commanders by alternative means. For visual or wireless signalling the code word PYE will mean "The advance will commence according to plan at ZERO plus 6 hours. AAA ACKNOWLEDGE

From: BUVU
Place:
Time:

* This line should be erased if not required.

150th Infantry Brigade
Operation Order No. 199   Copy No 5

Ref Map 57B 1/40,000   16 Oct 1918

1. The XIII Corps is attacking the enemy's position to-morrow, October 17th at an hour which will be communicated later.

2. The attack will be carried out in accordance with instructions that have already been issued (Instruction No. 2. para.1)

3. PLAN. At ZERO plus 3 hours the 7th Bn Wilts Regt followed by the 2nd Bn Royal Munster Fusiliers will move via Bridges in Q 28 A & C to position about Q 18 D.5.5 and Q 18.C.5.5 respectively. The 2nd Bn North'd Fus will move via ST. BENIN to about Q 12.C.0.4.

By ZERO plus 5½ hours the 7th Bn Wilts Regt & the 2nd Bn North'd Fus on Right & left respectively will be formed up behind the RED LINE with the 2nd Bn Royal Munster Fus in support, ready to attack through to the 2nd objective on receipt of orders from the G.O.C 150 Inf. Bde.

Objectives & dividing lines are shown on map issued to Bn Commanders.

4. MOPPING UP - O.C 2 Bn R Munster Fus will detail 2 Companies to mop up BASUEL.

5. CONSOLIDATION 7th Bn Wilts Regt will consolidate 2nd Objective in depth from right Divl Boundary to BASUEL POMMEREUIL road inclusive. 2nd Bn North'd Fus will consolidate 2nd objective from BASUEL-POMMEREUIL road exclusive to left Divl Boundary.

6. LIAISON POSTS Joint Liaison posts will be established:-

K.36.D.4.8. by 2nd Bn North'd Fus with 149 Inf Bde & 66 Divn

R.10.A.2.6 }
R.9.C.0.5 } by 7th Bn Wilts Rgt with 27th American Divn

R.14.B.0.6 by 2nd Bn R Muns Fus with 27th American Divn

7. ARTILLERY
1. Battery of 112 Bde RFA will work with 7th Bn Wilts Regt & 1 Batty 86th AFA Bde will work with 2nd Bn North'd Fus.

1.

8. **L.T.M.B.** - The 150th L.T.M. Batty will advance in rear of the 2nd Bn. R. Munster Fus. but will keep a liaison officer with the Hqrs 7th Bn. Welsh Regt. The battery will be prepared to assist the 7th Bn. Welsh Regt. in the assault on BASUEL.

9. **TANKS** - Tanks are co-operating in the attack of the 50th Divn.

10. **CONTACT PLANES** - Ref. Instructions No 2. para 3 (b) all men in front line will light a flare when called for & supplies of flares will be pushed up from the support companies.

11. **MACHINE GUNS**. Two sections machine guns will cover the advance of 150th Inf Bde to the 2nd objective.

12. Instructions re Headquarters, communications, medical and Administrative instructions have been issued already.

13. Watches will be synchronised by the Officers of 150th Inf. Bde. at ~~Battalion~~ HQs 2nd Bn. North'd Fus at 2200 hrs 16th instant. Units will send an Officer with a watch.

14. **ACKNOWLEDGE**

Issued at 1830 hrs
Thro Signals

J. A. Bryson
Captain
Bde. Major
150 Inf Brigade

HQ 150th Inf Bde
16th Oct. 1918

Copy No 1 G.O.C.
      2. S.C.
      3. 2d N. Fus
      4. 7th Welsh Regt
      5. 2d R Muns Fus
      6. 150 L.T.M. Batty
      7. 50 Division
      8. 149 Inf Bde
      9. 151 Inf Bde
     10. S.A. Bde
     11. 27 American Bde
     12. 50 Bn. M.G.C.
     13. 86 Bde R.F.A.
     14. 112 Bde R.F.A.
     15. File
     16. War Diary

150TH INFANTRY BRIGADE
OPERATION ORDER NO. 201.

Copy No. 6

28th October 1918.

Ref. Map. 57b. 1/40,000.

1. The 150th Infantry Brigade will move to LE CATEAU on the 29th instant by march route in accordance with march table attached.

2. Billeting parties will meet the Staff Captain at the CROSS Road K.33.a. at 11.00 hours 29th instant.

3. Supplies will be normal.

4. Battalions will send a watch to be sychronised at Brigade Headquarters at 08.30 hours 29th instant.

5. Brigade will move complete in personnel. Staff Captain will issue orders for storing of surplus kit and blankets.

6. Brigade Headquarters will close at MARETZ at 10.00 hrs. and open in CHATEAU SEYDOUX on arrival.

7. ACKNOWLEDGE.

Captain,
Brigade Major,
150th Infantry Brigade.

Issued at   hrs.
Thro' Signals.

Copy No. 1. G.O.C.
2. ?.?.
3. B.S.O.
4. 2nd Bn. North'd. Fus.
5. 7th Bn. Wilts. Regt.
6. 2nd Bn. R. Munster Fus.
7. 150th Trench Mortar Bty.
8. 50th Division.
9. 149th Inf. Brigade.
10. Area Commdt. MARETZ.
11. File.
12. War Diary.
13. Spare.
14. "

MARCH TABLE TO ACCOMPANY 150TH INFANTRY BRIGADE OPERATION ORDER NO.201.

Serial No.	UNIT.	Starting Point.	Time.	Route.	DESTINATION.	Remarks.
1.	2nd Bn. Royal Munster Fusiliers.	Railway Crossing. V.1.c.6.4.	hours 10.00.	BUSIGNY-	LE CATEAU	Distances to be maintained :-
2.	7th Bn. Wiltshire Regiment.	do.	10.15.	HONNECHY STATION-	do.	Between Coys - 100 yds. " Bns. - 500 " Between Units)- 100 " and Transport)
3.	2nd Bn. North'd. Fusiliers.	do.	10.26.	LE CATEAU.	do.	Between groups) - 25 " of 3 vehicles)
4.	150th L.T.Mortar Battery.	do.	10.39.		do.	Forward of HONNECHY STATION
5.	150th Inf.Brigade Headquarters.	do.	10.41.		do.	Between Coys - 200 yds. " Bns. - 1000 "

"A" Form
MESSAGES AND SIGNALS.

Army Form C.
(In pads of 100.)

No. of Message............

Prefix........Code........m.	Words	Charge.	This message is on a/c of :	Recd. at......m.
Office of Origin and Service Instructions	Sent			Date.............
....	At ....m.		..................Service.	From ....
....	To			
....	By		(Signature of "Franking Officer")	By...............

TO { GOTA
ROME
.... }

Sender's Number.	Day of Month.	In reply to Number.	AAA
BX. 34			

The Brigade will advance
on receipt of these orders
via bridges N. 5 S... R.E.
to ... bottled the ...
the railway ... R.... up to
... ...
of the ... of 29 ...
29 K... ... for the
support AAA Advanced Bde
H.Q. will be established at
junction of leading ... the
Q.29 up ... ...

South of Q 28 Central

From
Place
Time 0855

The above may be forwarded as now corrected. (Z)

Censor.   Signature of Addressor or person authorised to telegraph in his name
* This line should be erased if not required.

Order No. 1625   Wt. W3253/   P 511   27/2   H. & K., Ltd. (E. 2634).

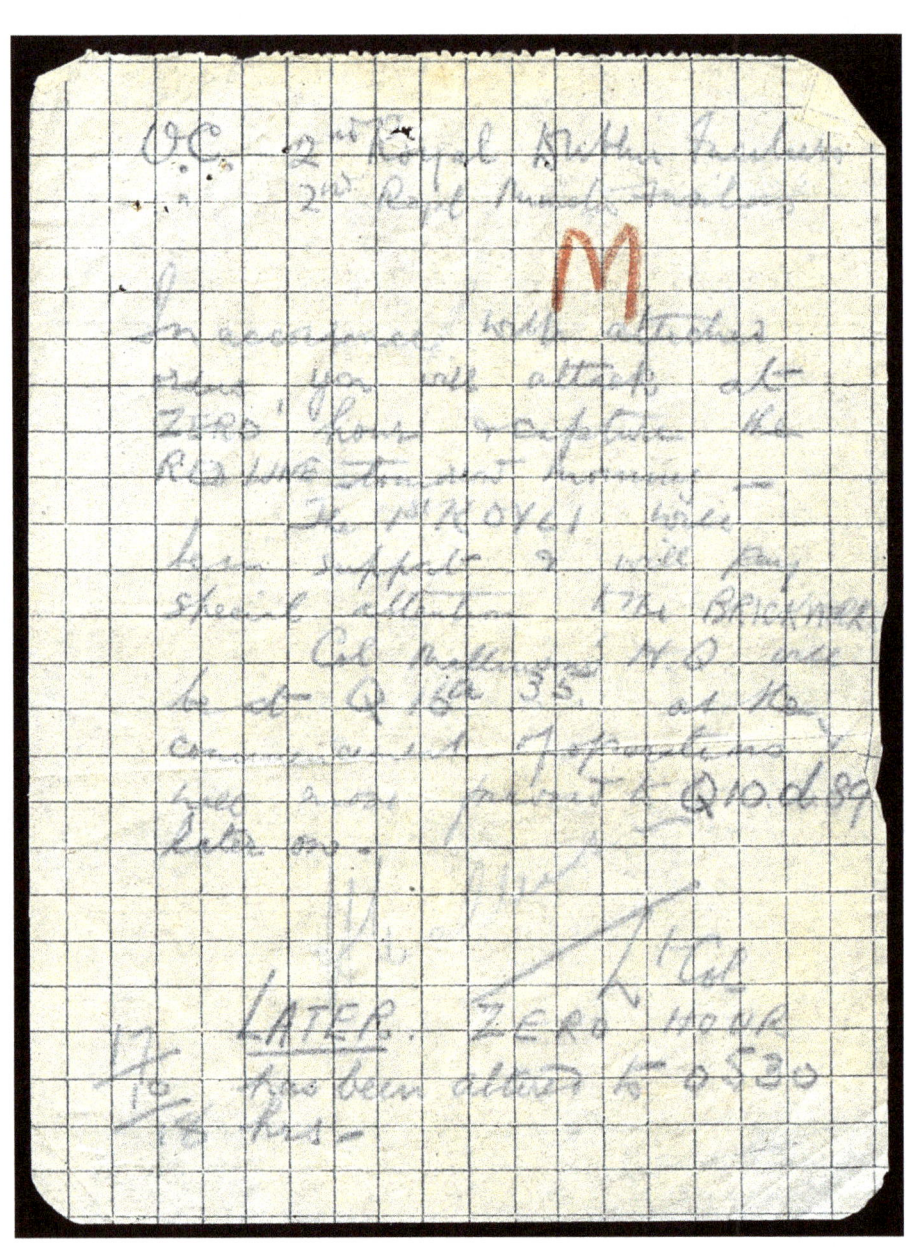

O.C. 2nd Royal Dublin Fusiliers
2nd Royal Munster Fusiliers

M

In conjunction with attached
arms you will attack at
ZERO hour & capture the
RED LINE from point passing
thro' M.KOV61 will
been support & will pay
special attention to the BRICKWK
Col Mallings H.Q. will
be at Q.16.a.3.5. at the
commencement of operations &
will move forward to Q.10.d.8.9
later on.

Lt Col

LATER. ZERO HOUR
has been altered to 0530
hrs.

MESSAGES AND SIG…

Prefix.............. Code.............. m.	Words	Charge.	This message is on a/c of:	Recd. at...
Office of Origin and Service Instructions	Sent		..........................Service.	Date..............
	At.................m. M			From ....
	To			
	By		(Signature of "Franking Officer")	By................

TO

Sender's Number.	Day of Month.	In reply to Number.	AAA

From

Place

Time

The above may be forwarded as now corrected. .... Censor.	(Z) .... Signature of Addressor or person authorised to telegraph in his name

* This line should be erased if not required.

Order No. 1625 Wt. W3253/ P 511 27/2 H. & K., Ltd. (E. 2634).

SECRET.   APPENDIX I   October 1918
                                              Secret
2ND. BATTN. THE ROYAL MUNSTER FUSILIERS.

NARRATIVE OF OPERATIONS OCTOBER 3rd. - 7th. 1918.

Reference Map MONTBREH IN 1/40,000 Edition 1.A.

BONY	3rd. October.	Received orders at 0200 hrs to march from EPEHY at 0330 hrs and take up position in trenches on N Side of GUILLEMONT FARM as Bde reserve, and were in position at 0600 hrs. At 1200 hrs moved up into HINDENBURG LINE, N of BONY. The 151st. Inf Bde who had attacked LE CATELET were driven back. At 1500 hrs "A" & "B" Coys took up position in CATELET Line S of village facing N. with left flank well thrown back. At 1830 hrs battn was ordered to take up line S of LE CATELET facing N. "A" Coy on right to S of GOUY. "B" Coy in the centre & "C" in touch with 149th. Inf Bde at MACQUINCOURT FARM. "D" Coy & H.Q. in reserve in sunken road S of LE CATELET. 2 Lt.J.J. CARSON wounded in arm by sniper S.E. of LE CATELET.
LE CATELET	4th. October.	At 0200 hrs the Commanding Officer was called to Bde H.Q. and received orders to attack LE CATELET and take LA PANNERIE SOUTH at 0610 hrs in conjunction with 3rd. Royal Fusiliers on the left; with two Coys of the 2nd. Northumberland Fusiliers to "mop up" Runners were at once sent to Coy Commanders to attend Battn. H.Q. and for the battn to assemble at the same time on "B" Coy in the following order - First two waves "A" & "B" Coy with a frontage of 450 yards each. "C" Coy to form 3rd wave, and "D" Coy 4th wave.- A very difficult operation & well carried out considering the ground had not been reconnoitred or seen by daylight. Fairly heavy shelling going on all the time the battn moved forward at 0600 hrs in order to pick up with the barrage, which commenced at 0610 hrs on a line three quarters of the way through the village. The battn suffered very heavy casualties from machine gun nests in the village, but managed to force its way through and gain the rising ground immediately to N. Here "A" Coy lost direction and got on to lower slopes of PROSPECT HILL, and did not join with battn, until after the objective had been taken. "C" Coy came under very heavy T.M. & M.G. fire from their left owing to the fact that the North'd Fus had failed to keep up with the battn. 2 Lt.R.V.FLANAGAN, although twice wounded managed to lead his platoon close up to our objective, when he was wounded a third time & stuck to his post until night fall when he was relieved. "D" Coy, in Battn reserve, forced its way through the centre of the village, through the gap left by "A" & "B" Coys until they were held up in N end of village by 2 M.G. nests. Eventually these nests were ejected by the approach of one of our parties, attracted by the sound of the Commanding Officers hunting horn, and the battn was able to work up LE CATELET trench without very much opposition and took their objective at 0945 hrs, which was consolidated and held, until relieved the following day.

LE CATELET contd.	4th. October.	Hdqr Coy which had lost touch was ordered at 1200 hrs to fill up gap between ourselves, and the 7th. WILTS Regt on the right. At about 1300.Detachments of "B" & "C" Coys which had become detached from rest of battn & had been compelled to withdraw to CATELET line S. of LE CATELET, were reorganised under Capt. C.C.SMYTHE & Capt. A.KEEVIL,M.B.E. M.C. Acting under instructions received from Bde H.Q. "C" Coy attempted to force their way up CATELET trench between LE CATELET & GOUY to rejoin C.O. in LA PANNERIE SOUTH trench system - One Platoon of "C" Coy got through & remainder owing to casualties withdrew to S of village. "B" Coy proceeded under Capt;C.C.Smythe, in accordance with verbal instructions, round E of GOUY & Western slopes of PROSPECT HILL & rejoined remainder of Bn under C.O. The remains of "C" Coy followed half an hour after "B" Coy round E side of Gouy. At dusk three attacks were organised to clear up our left flank, i.e. (1) in a Northerly direction from A.4.central (2) in a westerly direction from LE CATELET trench (by K.O.Y.L.I. under orders O.C. 2 R Munster Fus) (3) by "D" Coy in a South Westerly direction to enemy trenches in S.29. This attack was successfully carried out and left flank made secure. The trenches held by the battn were heavily shelled in the afternoon, and Lieut. C.M.J.RYAN.M.C. was killed.
LA PANNERIE SOUTH	5th.October.	At 0200 rations arrived. At 0500 got orders for relief, and by 0630 were relieved by South Wales Bord. and went back to dugouts in railway embankment at GOUY. - slight shelling in morning. In afternoon "C" & "D" occupied trenches in front of PROSPECT HILL, with "A"Coy in support. "B" Coy sent out parties to search for wounded- bring in dead - & salvage. About 1700 hrs got heavily shelled by H.E. & "Mustard" gas, and several men sent to hospital owing to eyes being affected.
GOUY	6th;October.	About 0830 hrs orders received to attack BEAUREVOIR LINE. 115th. Inf Bde on our left, 7th. Wilts on right. "C" & "D" Coys formed first two waves. "A" Coy third wave, "B" Coy in reserve. One platoon of "D" Coy under Lieut.E.D.CONRAN.M.C. occupied trenches in front of GUISENCOURT FARM. The battn forced its way up to enemy wire, in spite of very heavy M.G. fire from prepared emplacements. Capt.J.O'BRIEN.M.C. was killed trying to get through the wire, and Capt.V.D. O'MALLEY.(A/Adjt). Capt.A/KEEVIL.M.B.E. M.C. & Lieut.E.B.RUSSELL were wounded. About 1730 hrs orders were received by the battn to be relieved by the 2nd. R.Dublin Fus. and the battn marched back to BONY by Coys by 2230 hrs.
BONY	7th.October.	Cleaning up. The battn under one hours notice to move.

APPENDIX II   SECRET   H.Q., 150TH INFANTRY BRIGADE.

150TH INFANTRY BRIGADE.

NARRATIVE OF OPERATIONS 16TH OCTOBER, 1918.

October 16th. The front held by the 150th Infantry Brigade from Q.9.c.8.3. to Q.27.d.5.5. was taken over by the 149th Infantry Brigade on the left and the 151st Infantry Brigade on the right. Battalions of the 150th Infantry Brigade were withdrawn about 2:00 and came into reserve.

October 17th. At Zero hour, 0520 hours, the 150th Infantry Brigade was disposed - Bde. Hd.Qrs. - HONNECHY STATION, 2nd Bn. North'd Fusiliers Sunken Road Q.19.a. - 2nd Bn. Royal Munster Fusiliers - sunken road Q.26.a. - 7th Bn. Wiltshire Regt. - sunken roads Q.26.b. and c. - 150th T.M.B. - Q.19.a.

The attack was carried out by the 151st Infantry Brigade, supported by the 149th Infantry Brigade.

The mist was very dense between Zero hour and about 1000 hours.

About 0930 it appeared that the 151st Infantry Brigade had reached their objective (the line of road in Q.17 and 23) on the right, but on the left fighting was still taking place on the line of the railway. About 1000 hours the 150th Infantry Brigade were ordered to move up to the line of the Railway in Q.28. At 1115 hours the Brigade was disposed - Bde. Hd.Qrs. on railway embankment Q.28.c. 2nd Bn. North'd Fusiliers - Q.28.a. 7th Bn. Wiltshire Regt. with 2nd Bn. R. Munster Fusiliers in close support in Q.28.c. The G.O.C. 150th Infantry Brigade ordered a general advance to the Red Line to commence at 1230, but counter orders were received from the Division and the Brigade were ordered to stand fast while the G.O.C. returned to Q.19 central to receive instructions from the Divisional Commander. An advanced Bde. Report Centre under Lieut. W.H. GRIFFITHS, 2nd Bn. North'd Fusiliers, was left on the railway embankment. This Advanced Bde. Hd.Qrs. was in touch with Bde. Hd.Qrs. by phone and was found invaluable.

About 1500 hours the 7th Bn. Wiltshire Regt. were ordered to occupy the high ground in Q.28.b. to support the 4th K.R.R.C. who were being forced back. About 1600 hours the Divisional front was regrouped. The G.O.C. 150th Infantry Brigade was allotted the 7th Bn. Wiltshire Regt., 3rd Royal Fusiliers and 4th K.R.R.C. and ordered to make good the line of the road from right Divisional boundary in Q.23.d. to ORCHARD Q.17.c. The 7th Bn. Wiltshire Regt. occupied this line after dusk without opposition. The centre sector was allotted to the 151st Infantry Brigade and the left sector to the 149th Infantry Brigade.

The 2nd Bn. Royal Munster Fusiliers and 2nd Bn. North'd Fusiliers passed to command of 151st Infantry Brigade and 149th Infantry Brigade respectively.

Sheet 2.

October 18th. At 0530 the attack was recommenced under an artillery barrage with the object of capturing the RED LINE (1st objective). On the 150th Infantry Brigade front the attack was carried out by the 7th Bn. Wiltshire Regt. with the 3rd Royal Fusiliers in close support. The advance was checked on the right on the line of the sunken road in Q.19.a. by machine gun fire from ROUX FARM, with the left LA swung up into the orchards in Q.18.d.

At Zero plus the 75th Infantry Brigade passed through the 7th Bn. Wiltshire Regt. but advanced only a short distance.

About 1200 hours the enemy took away the machine gun from LA ROUX FARM and a joint post of R.W.F. and Americans was established there.

About 1500 hours the 75th Infantry Brigade recommenced their advance into BASUEL and the 7th Bn. Wiltshire Regt. swung up their left flank to keep touch with the right of the 75th Infantry Brigade.

All Battalions stood fast during the night 18/19th.

October 19th. All Units of the 150th Infantry Brigade were withdrawn from the line about 1200 and proceeded to billets in MARETZ.

APPENDIX II

Officers of Batt'n present at
LE CATELET Action 3rd–7th Oct 1918.

Lieut. Col. H.B. Torson Rye DSO.

Captain   A.B. Holt   (Liason off. at 150 Bde HQ).
   "   J. O'Brien   MC.   (killed)
   " +adjt U.D. O'Malley MC.   (wounded)
   "   E.R.H. Orford MC. (wounded)
   "   A. Keirnl   MC MBE. (wounded)
   "   C.E. Smythe
   "   J.F.C. Haslam MC. RAMC.

Lieut   E.R. Hudson   (wounded).
   "   A.L.B. Stevens   (wounded - at duty)
   "   C.M.J. Ryan   MC.   (killed).
   "   T. Roche   (Tpt off.)
   "   W. McKewon   (wounded)
   "   C.T. Baldwin   (wounded)
   "   E.D. Connor   MC.
   "   R.L. Philpot   (wounded)

2 Lieut   P.J. Farrell.
   "   D. Minahan
   "   R.V. Hanagan   (wounded)
   "   E.B. Russell   (wounded)
   "   J.J. Carson   (wounded)
   "   J. King   (killed)
   "   P.S. Ahearne   (wounded)
   "   D. Daly   (killed)

24-10-18

Officers present at action on 18/10/18
between LE CATEAU & BAZUEL

Captain C.R. Williams M.C.   Cmdg Bn
"   S.W. Whateley   (wounded)
"   /a/jt A.B. Holt
"   T.E. Toller
"   T.F.C. Haslam M.C. R.A.M.C.

Lieut   A.L.B. Stevens
"   F.J. O'Farrell
"   T. Roche   (Tpt. O/R)

2Lieut   J.R. Howe   (killed)
"   H.G. Carolin   (wounded)
"   D. Minahan   (wounded)
"   H.W. Clarke   (wounded)
"
"

24/10/18   A.B. Holt Capt
                            a/ajt 2/RMF

150/50

Army Form C. 2118.

WAR DIARY
or
INTELLIGENCE SUMMARY.
(Erase heading not required.)

2nd Royal Munster Fusiliers

Nov 4 6

Place	Date	Hour	Summary of Events and Information	Remarks and references to Appendices
LE CATEAU	1/11/18		In billets. 15/15 Bn parade on which G.O.C. 50th Div presented immediate awards to 2nd Cpl Ewing, 9112 CSM Tyree, 2568 Sgt O'Gorman, 811 Pte Williams, 5265 Pte McCarthy.	*note*
LE CATEAU	2/11/18		Some shelling of Le Cateau during night 1/2nd Nov.	*note*
		1030	C.O, Coy Comdrs Intelligence Officer proceeded by car to Bousies to reconnoitre assembly area for 4/11/18.	*note*
LE CATEAU	3/11/18	0910	C.O. sent for to attend at Bde S.Q. to explain plan arrangement of operations to GOC 50 Bde.	*note*
			Capt Livingston proceeded to Bt. H.Q. to interview Tank Commander.	*note*
		1330	Bn HQ moved out of billets to bivouac area near Pommereuil. Bn Mess.	*note*
			Surplus moved to other billets in Le Cateau. Following awarded bar to M.M. No 5787 L/Cpl T. Kennedy, "C" Coy - Awarded military medal No 6028 Pte Carroll M. & No 6436 Pte T. Stokes & No 29302 Pte Burke R. & No 4053 Sgt Paver W.L. awarded DCM	*note* 130th Bde I.3.0am 2nd
POMMEREUIL	4/11/18		The Battalion moved to FONTAINE-au-BOIS at 01.30. Hy had and Afternoon Lillies were heavily shelled and A Coy had 3 casualties. Zero hour was 0.5.15. B Coy advanced immediately behind the the creeping barrage in rear of the 2nd NF. and followed to Waft	*note* B
and FONTAINE				
au BOIS				

WAR DIARY

NOVEMBER 1918.

2nd Royal Munster Fus

Place	Date	Hour	Summary of Events and Information	Remarks and references to Appendices
FONTAINE AU-BOIS	4.11.18		At a portion of the Forest of MORMAL this they accomplished by 13.00 when they arrived in the Hunters trench situated approximately south east of Fontaine. The wood was thick and held by machine gun posts.	
			A Company under Capt Livingston with C Coy on its left Flank met the 3 Tanks in the trenches road at 12:50. After June and pressed to their objective PREUX-AUX-BOIS up the new country to the west of the Road of Mormal at Fontaine au Bois being placed on the Rd. Few prisoners being taken. Casualties were light.	SAM
			But there were eventually April 14 and 2 Livings to be dispatched forth to 18th Division. Capt. Livingston met our liason of the "Bedfords" to the village of PREUX of 13.15 soon after the linking of the two Battns which had been advancing towards each other. At 14.30 WBt Livings's border was consolidated and all the enemy trench to up and lines in posts established. Part of Cambrai was fed their wounds the wind to the morning and did all join up till next they The Battalion/bivouacked in the sunken road and marched to the junction of the ROUTE DE FONTAINE and the light division in the FOREST DE MORMAL where they bivouacked for the night the casualties for the	(A 186)

NOVEMBER 1918
2nd Royal Munster Fus.

WAR DIARY or **INTELLIGENCE SUMMARY**
(Erase heading not required.)
Army Form C. 2118.

Place	Date	Hour	Summary of Events and Information	Remarks and references to Appendices
FOREST DE MORMAL	4·11·18	1600	Day's fighting was as follows (since issued warrant) 2/Lt H.R. Clarke & 2/Lt A. Stirling wounded. Other Ranks killed 16 wounded 59. R.P. O'B	C
FOREST de MORMAL	5·11·18		The morning was wet and cold and rations were delayed as the railhead had been moved up, but they arrived at 04.30 & Battalion moved at 0700 and halted in the Forêt de Mormal for dinner. The Battalion marched by easy	
RUE DES TUIFS	5·11·18 to 6·11·18	1700	at 1500 to RUE DES TUIFS. The bridge across the SAMBRE had been blown up and was in course of reconstruction. It was not until able to get across till the morning of the 6th [crossed out] 24 Brigade [crossed out]	
RUE DES TUIFS	6·11·18		The Battalion left RUE DES TUIFS at 0630 with A Company as advance guard. On arriving at NOYELLE bridge it was found to have been blown up and the village held by the enemy. The 4th & 5th had sent 5 Platoons over the river higher up & were to attack NOYELLES from the North but before they had not turned up. However Capt Livingston decided to get across the river, and by being his last C. to either flank of the NOYELLE Rd commanded the river, he was able to get his Company across. The enemy field guns were shelling the road but by using the west side of the road. Lieut Guerin there able to get to the	D

NOVEMBER 1918 — 2nd ROYAL MUNSTER FUS.

WAR DIARY / INTELLIGENCE SUMMARY
Army Form C. 2118.

Place	Date	Hour	Summary of Events and Information	Remarks and references to Appendices
FONTAINE au BOIS	6/11/18	8 am	3rd R.M.F. (at Croixwalk a small serve) River and cross the river "Aunelle" to proceeded to clear the village of NOYELLE and then advanced up the main road to PREUX CHAPELLE. Clearing the road on each side, about 60 prisoners and many wounded Huns were captured. Coys. had been wheeled to reorganise on the sunken road N of PREUX CHAPELLE and were ready to push on with the	
PREUX CHAPELLE		11.30	Battalion. 2nd R.M.F. The Battalion received their Baptême of firing with the 2nd R.M.F. and 4th hills on the road behind. A meeting of the O.C. R.M.F. 2nd R.M.F. & 8th Leinster's Nova' and the 3rd R. Fusiliers being an excellent example of His Liaison. They were noticeable during the tour of the operation, the artillery, Trench Mortar and Machine gun fire, the check to each until were also heavy. His dispositions of the way advance which was due then, was as follows. The 3rd R. Fusiliers on left. With the Leinsters in their right. The 2nd R.M.F. on Munster's right and the Munsters on the 2nd M.F. right front. Now a good deal of delay in getting the units into their proper line, the hills here kept cold, as it had been raining all day, the enemy who at firing occupied the wood in the direct line of attack	

WAR DIARY
INTELLIGENCE SUMMARY.
(Erase heading not required.)

Army Form C. 2118.

November 1918

2/1 Royal Munster Fusiliers

Place	Date	Hour	Summary of Events and Information	Remarks and references to Appendices
	6/11/8		fired a few bursts of M.G. & T.M. fire on the vicinity of the Baily.	
		1330	The advance commenced at 1330 — No opposition was met and we advanced with "A" on the right "B" on the left & "C" in support. Through the BOIS DU DIABLE farm where we captured a field gun. When we approached the AVESNES — LEURS railway close to the village of JEAN LEDOUX we encountered heavy M.G. fire and also fire from a field gun at point blank range, we here marched time to get touch with our flanks. On our left we had lost touch altogether with the Scottish Horse, who from the firing seemed to be encountering stubborn resistance & to be not so advanced as we. It was decided to advance on our objective which was the road running N. & S. through the village of ST REMY CHAUSSÉE. As soon as we advanced we were met with a terrific M.G. fire and were unable to advance to our final objective, taking cover in a sunken road (B19 C). The enemy's fire suddenly ceased and patrols reported that the enemy had retired "A" & "B" Coys then advanced to their objective and went into billets with outposts thrown out well forward. Touch was obtained with the Scottish Horse on the road on our left & with the 2/North. Fus. at LA CHAPELLE	ASD

WAR DIARY

2nd ROYAL MUNSTER Fus.

NOVEMBER 1918

Army Form C. 2118.

INTELLIGENCE SUMMARY.
(Erase heading not required.)

Instructions regarding War Diaries and Intelligence Summaries are contained in F.S. Regs., Part II. and the Staff Manual respectively. Title pages will be prepared in manuscript.

Place	Date	Hour	Summary of Events and Information	Remarks and references to Appendices
S. REMY CHAUSSEE	6.11	16.00	Att on their preserve line with out-posts starting well forward. C Company were in support. The enemy shelled our line with much motored high velocity shells during the night. Casualties were other ranks killed 3 and wounded 10.	II
S. REMY CHAUSSEE	7.11		The enemy continued to shell us during the morning paying special attention to the cross roads. It was at 0700 that 2/Lt. Nisbet with No 11 & B Company was killed whilst endeavouring his men to trenches in front of moving to the increased shelling. H.Q. now moved into billets at PREMY CHAUSSÉE. The enemy continued a shelling the village during the day and night with 5.9s. But we only had 5 O.Rs wounded. The 157 Bde passed through the 150 Bde and took up the pursuit.	L
		1300	Battle of Sambre. Aff LE CATEAU at 1300 and arrived at LANDRECIES at 16.30	

NOVEMBER 1918

WAR DIARY
2nd ROYAL MUNSTER FUS.
INTELLIGENCE SUMMARY

Army Form C. 2118.

Place	Date	Hour	Summary of Events and Information	Remarks and references to Appendices
S. REMY CHAUSSÉE	8.11		The Battalion remained at ST REMY CHAUSSEE in billets, the enemy shelled H.Q. till 11.00. The Bde. was formed into 3 mobile columns under the command of the 3 O.C. Battalions, each column had Artillery, one section French Mortar and one M.G. Section attached to it. The column under O.C. 2nd R M F to advance through FLAURSIES, the column under OC 3rd N.F. to advance through MONTPLAISIERS, and the column under OC 2nd R.M.F. to advance through SEMOUSIES, but the scheme was vetoed by the Army. The 149 Bde. attained their objective namely the Bois de BEUGNIES. 3 O.Rs. killed 6 and 7 Coy R.F. from Battle Dublin. Left TAWDRECIES at 7300 and arrived LACHAPELLE 1830	
	9.11		The Battalion marched to SARS-POTERIES which was reached at 14.30. We were billeted the inhabitants who were delighted to have the inhabitants who could act as guides for the English troops who were the first troops to enter the town since the Battle of MONS 1914. Five trains and a big Ammunition dumps were captured at SARS POTERIES. We were went into billets	G [large letter] 10th IRI No 7 B.M. 793

WAR DIARY 2nd ROYAL MUNSTER FUS.
INTELLIGENCE SUMMARY

NOVEMBER 1918

Place	Date	Hour	Summary of Events and Information	Remarks and references to Appendices
SARS POTERIES	10.11.18		The Battalion moved from SARS POTERIES to DOULIERS DOULIERS where they arrived at 15:30 and went into billets. Battle further OWN up from ST CHAPELLE and joined the Battalion. The reports of delayed mines at the Cross Roads were heard during the night.	H
DOURLERS	11.11.18		Were received that hostilities would cease two sentenced about 9:30 a.m. 2 Lt Freeman joined the Battalion.	
DOURLERS	12.11.18		An R.C. Service was held at 10.30 at H.Q. A Lt memorial Service was held the HQ & 150 Bns here present and addresses to were delivered by the General Y. theoret. The following appeared in part II Orders of Bn. - A Reginald M.E. her F Me LIEUT. E.D. CONRANNEY M.C. T. O'MALLEY M.O. ATHEATRA CAPT. O.C. SMYTHE (Maine and) 2nd Lt FLANAGAN awarded M.C. Sgt PAULKEY No. 7033 awarded D.C.M by the Marshal C-in-Chief	

WAR DIARY
or
INTELLIGENCE SUMMARY

NOVEMBER 1918   2nd ROYAL MUNSTER FUS   Army Form C. 2118.

Place	Date	Hour	Summary of Events and Information	Remarks and references to Appendices
DOULLERS	13th		Coy Parades the wearing of S.B.Rs and steel helmets was then continued	
"	14th		Parades as usual. Lieut-Col Regan took over Command of 13 Brigade. The inspection of all Battalion equipment was also carried out.	
"	15th		Parades as usual. Part of the Battalion working on ammunition dump at SRS POTERIES. The following awards appeared in the Gazette. Lt.Col. Ireton Fry - D.S.O., Capt. N.B. Holt. Lieut. F. O'Farrell, Lieut. P. Roche M.C. and No.20385 Pte J.E. Kent D.C.M.	
"	16th		Ceremonial Parade under the R.S.M. Work on ammunition dump under Lieut Col E.E. Fellan DSO visited the Battalion.	
"	17th		Church Parades. 2nd Lieut O'Connor & 2nd Lieut Burges joined the Bn from U.K. and D. for/afternoon	
"	18th		Parades under R.S.M. Head Quarter Company was attended Capt. Maltin M.C. the Battalion M.O. left at 2 hours notice to join the 1st Army. Capt. Linough took over 2nd in Command of Battalion, Captain Maguire took over Adjy and Capt. Rennie took over story	

WAR DIARY
INTELLIGENCE SUMMARY

Army Form C. 2118.

Place	Date	Hour	Summary of Events and Information	Remarks and references to Appendices
DOULERS	19th		The Battalion moved to THISNIERS where the Bn went into billets. 2nd Lt. Murphy reported from 3rd R.M.F. (U.K.)	K
THISNIERS	20th		Three Companies were employed in salvage work and one Company carried on with training. 2nd Lt. Hilyard reported from U.K. with 97 O.R's	
"	21st		The Arsenal Cars and a Lorry were placed at the disposal of the Battalion to visit ETREUX, the Scene of the 2nd Bn's fight in August 1914. Major Williams M.C. Capt Fitzm. M.O and Lieut Smith with R.S.M. Reynolds and Q.M.S. Trevisi and two men who were with the Battalion in August 1914 visited Hauvarnes (?) little Chapotinie. The movements of the Battalion from FERGNY Cross-Roads to ETREUX were followed with the help of Mr Victor Rickard. The graves of Buchan soldiers were found in the Cemetery at FESMY and also three in ETREUX Cemetery, the orchard where the 2nd Bn. made their last stand at FERGNY was also found with the two graves the with 113 men and the two Crosses the Germans had put a railing round them, but one with 9 officers, The Germans had put a railing round them, but	

NOVEMBER 1918.

WAR DIARY 2nd Royal Munster

INTELLIGENCE SUMMARY.

Place	Date	Hour	Summary of Events and Information	Remarks and references to Appendices
TAISNIERS	21st		The working on the ORVs was much obstructed, two new Crosses were erected which we had brought with us.	
"	22nd		Salvage work was continued. 2nd Lt R.C. Kent returned from Hospital for Duty. were available for the new under Battalion arrangements	
"	23		Salvage work was continued. Educational Scheme published for men who wanted to go after the war. Capt Irving took charge of the information Bureau	
"	24		Church Parade. The following Honours and Awards here granted No 8576 C.S.M. Murphy, Bar to M.M. No 8022 L/Cpl Murphy M.M. No 2602 Pte Laurence No 3994 Pte Boggs No 18607 Pte Medley No 3815 Sgt Mullinger No 20126 Sgt Grummond No 5990 Cpl Tobit No7074 L Sgt Burke the M.M.	
"	25th		Salvage work was continued. The following Honours Awards was granted No 9065 Sgt Griffin D.C.M. No 9a 1577 to C.Q.M.S 10734 No 5931 Sgt Clancey D.C.M.	

WAR DIARY 2nd ROYAL MUNSTER R. FUS

INTELLIGENCE SUMMARY

NOVEMBER 1918.

Army Form C. 2118.

Place	Date	Hour	Summary of Events and Information	Remarks and references to Appendices
TAISNIERS	26th		Salvage work continued. The Divisional Commander interviewed billets, transport and interior economy of Battalion. The following honours and awards were gratuled N° 200032 A/Cpl Fox N° 200689 A/Cpl Heff. N° 5334 Pte Hurd the M.M.	
"	27th		Inspection of billets by M.O. Football competition between Companies was started	
"	28th		Lt. Col. Braine L.O. posted the Battalion a route march of 24 hours was undertaken.	
"	29th		Inspection by Coys. were carried out. The following officers joined the Battalion 2/Lieuts H.G. Byrne, J.F. Luke, T.W. Marshall, R. Bushby M.M., P. Ryder	
"	30th		A practice Chemical parade took place at DOMPIERRE in anticipation of the Kings inspection of the 60th Division. The following officers reported their arrival Capt. Gibson M.C. and took over command of D Coy. 2/Lt Goodman and 2/Lt Asher.	

C.H.F. Milne (?)
Cmdg. 2/ Royal Munster (?)

Officers with Battle
Surplus of Battalion

Captain Hoft.   HQ
Captain Toller.   C
Lieut Stevens   HQ
Lieut F. O'Farrell C
2/Lieut Guerins.   A.
Lieut Regium.   B
Capt Morrissey   R.C. Padre

from November 3rd
to November 10th 1918.

B

The following Officers went into the line with the Battalion on November 3rd, 1918.

Head Quarters Major Williams MC
      Lieut Tarrant
      Lieut Maguier

A Coy
      Capt Livingston
  (K.) 2/Lieut Stone
    2/Lieut Harley

B Coy (K.) Lieut J.C. Dodd
     2/Lieut Edgar
  (W) 2/Lieut H.R. Clarke
  (W) 2/Lieut Dowling

C Coy Lieut Rathborne
    2/Lieut Jodrell
    2/Lieut Nash
    Lieut Sheffield

11

Captain Haslam M.C. M.O.
Lieut. T. Roche   Transport Off.
Captain Cotter   R.C. Chaplain

"A" Form.
MESSAGES AND SIGNALS.

Army Form C. 2121.
(In pads of 100.)

Prefix......Code......m.	Words.	Charge.	This message is on a/c of:	Recd. at......m.
Office of Origin and Service Instructions.	Sent			Date............
....	At........m.		..............Service.	From............
....	To............			
....	By............		(Signature of "Franking Officer.")	By............

TO			

Sender's Number.	Day of Month.	In reply to Number.	
BX 70	5		AAA

R/ Party Bn will not advance [illegible]
of the point [illegible] BX 29 the RWF
will [illegible] the [illegible]
about [illegible] TNB AB 6 45
[illegible] BX 7
and [illegible] 75 [illegible]

From: BWV
Place:
Time:

"A" Form
MESSAGES AND SIGNALS.

Army Form C. 2121 (in pads of 100).

Sender's Number.	Day of Month.	In reply to Number.	AAA
CO 45	5/4/18		

enter wood and dig
in A Company will
form vanguard leaving A28c87
at 06.50 hrs main
guard one section MGC
B.C. and H.Q. Coy and TMKA
200 yards will be
maintained between vanguard
and main guard
O.C. advance guard will
march at head of
main guard
Acknowledge

From / Place / Time: a/adj ...

"A" Form
MESSAGES AND SIGNALS.

Army Form C. 2121 (in pads of 100).

This message is on a/c of
6/150 T.M.B.
T.M.B. Coy

TO: H.Q. Coy, 9 File, 10 T.O.

Sender's Number.	Day of Month.	In reply to Number.	
C.T.45	5/11/18		AAA

150th Inf. Bde will move at 0700 about B.20.c order of march. Advance guard NUW1 and one section M.G.C. Company limbers six rear of their Companies remainder of echelon to in rear of column under Senior Transport officer Route la Currier Wvier A.20.a.3.9 Rue du Pontrouter to B.20.e.29 B.20.a.c Hot meats will be ready at this point Troops on will got remain arr the road but

Place: a/adj NUW1

"A" Form
MESSAGES AND SIGNALS.

Army Form C. 2121
(in pads of 100).

B

Day of Month: 4/11

AAA

Bde will be established at A28.c.2.?
Has the Bde will dispose in our
area about two points tonight
with an outpost posn to
throw out to the sea. AAA Ruby
will be responsible for left N.E. to
the rd junc at A28 d 9.0 — xrd AAA
Cota from B28 d 9.0. Inclusive to
Q14.4.1 incl Rgue & 57 T.M.
and A Coy M.G. both tele at our
area to the west of the factory
& Bivac A
Units will notify their area to
Bde HQ. and attach a runner to
runner with Bde HQ. AAA
Ack.

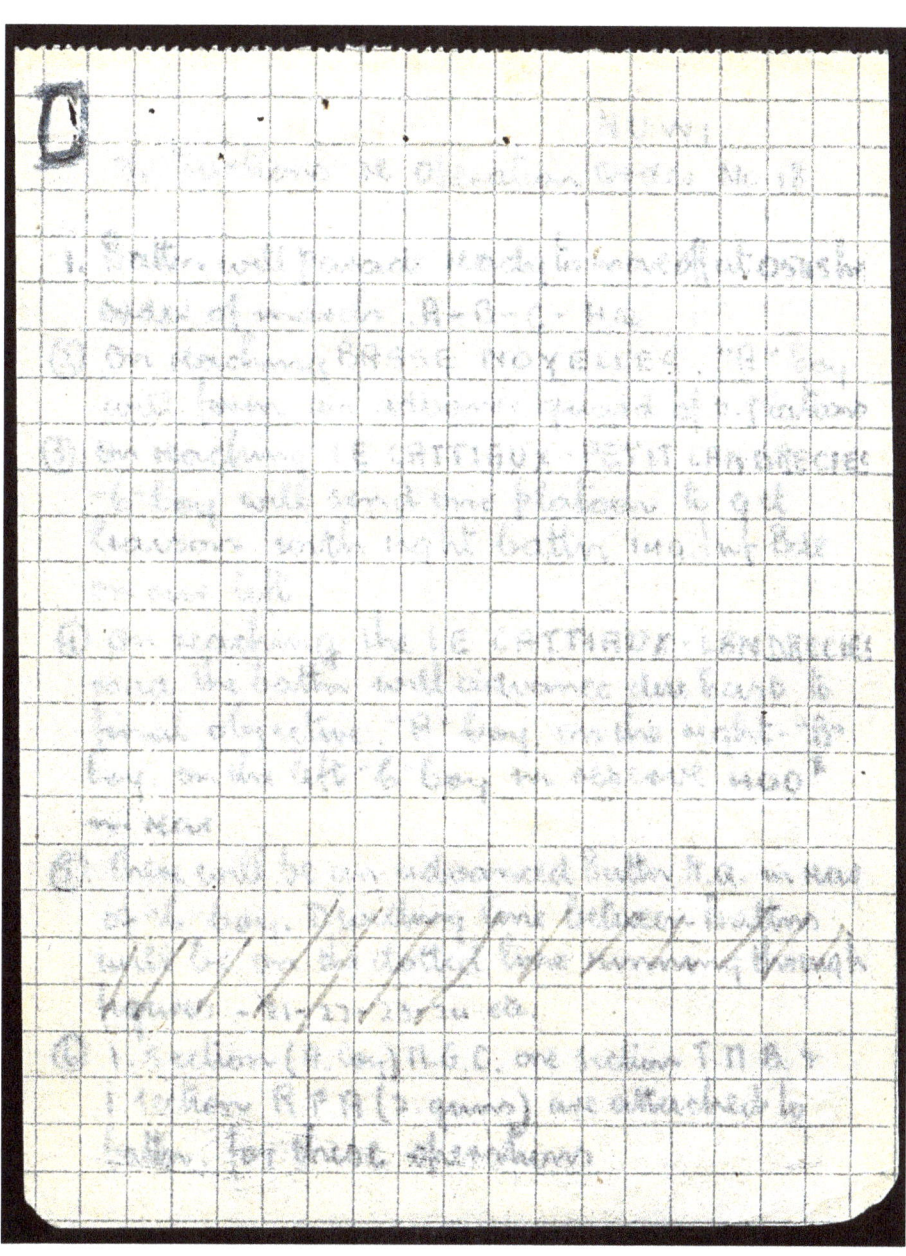

S.B. 22

```
 HQ 43
A  83
B  83
C  77
  ―――
  286
```

```
286
 22
―――
264
```

"A" Form
MESSAGES AND SIGNALS.

H

TO: 2th RMF

* 13 x 3. 9 AAA

60th Inf Bde & attached troops will move to DONLIERS after dinner tomorrow AAA Billetting parties will report to Div HQ at 1000 hrs tomorrow AAA

Ack.

From: 60th Inf Bde.

MESSAGES AND SIGNALS.

TO 2nd R. M F

Sender's Number: B6246
Day of Month: 9
AAA

The Germans have retired 180th Inf Bde Mobile Column will follow AAA 7th Wilts will pass xroads O 17 C 9 6 (St AUBIN) at 0900 hrs 9th followed by 5th NF and 2nd Rhers All Bns will move complete AAA TMs will follow Bns.
ack

From: 180th Inf Bde
Place:
Time:

Censor: H Tyson

SECRET.  2nd Bn. The Royal Munster Fusiliers.   Copy No. 3.

1/40,000   OPERATION ORDER NO. 22.   18/11/18.
57A Sheet.

1. The Bde will move to billets in TAISNIERES area tomorrow.

2. Battn will parade in marching order at 0850 hrs tomorrow.
   Order of march D. C. B. A. Coy. Transport, head of column at
   Orderly Room on N - side of road. Battn passes the church at 0900
   hrs following 150 Bde H.Q.

3. INSTRUCTIONS.
   (a) Full marching order will be worn. Jerkins will be carried outside
       & on top of the pack.
   (b) S.D. Caps will be worn - Steel Helmets will be was carried on
       the back of the pack.
   (c) No mess tins, mugs etc. will be carried hung from the
       equipment.
   (d) Blankets will be rolled in bundles of 10 and taken to the Q.M.Store
       by 0800.   Officers kits to be at H.Q. Officers Mess by 0800.
   (e) Certificates that billets have been left clean will be rendered
       before the Battn moves off.
   (f) Billeting Parties.   C.Q.M.S. will meet 2/Lieut O'Connor at
       Orderly Room 0800 to proceed to billeting area. This party
       will go on bicycles.

   (g) Further orders will be issued as to order of march of Transport
       when received from Bde.

                                              H. B. H O L T, Captain,
                                   A/Adjt 2nd Bn. The Royal Munster Fusiliers.

Issued at
        hrs

No.1.Copy War Diary.
   2   File.
   3   C.O.
   4   A Coy.
   5   B Coy.
   6   C Coy.
   7   D Coy.
   8   Transport Officer.
   9   Qr. Mr.
  10   R.S.M.

Reference para 2 of above.   A distance of 100 yds will be
maintained between Coys and between Battn & Transport.

Transport will march in rear of Battn.

SECRET 13   Copy No. 2

2ND BATTALION THE ROYAL MUNSTER FUSILIERS.
OPERATION ORDERS. NO. 17.   3rd Nov 1918

Reference Map France Sheet 57/N.W./1/20,000.

(1). **INFORMATION & INTENTION**
(a). The 150th Infantry Brigade with the 149th Inf Bde on its Right will take the First Objective tomorrow, 4th inst. Objectives already shewn to Coy Commdrs and marked on their Maps.
The 155st Inf Bde will take the second objective.
(b). The 7th Wilts will attack on the Right. 2nd Northd Fus will attack on the Left. The 2nd Roy Mun Fusiliers will Mop up, afterwards coming into Bde Reserve.

2. **DISTRIBUTION.**
(a). B.Coy 2nd Roy Mun Fus will advance 10 minutes behind rear Coy of 2nd Northd Fus, proceeding to G.3.a.7.5. thence patrolling the rides running North from G.3.b.3.7.-G.3.b.5.8.- A.27.d.9.2.-A.28.c.5.5. between the ROUTE DE FONTAINE and the LAIE DE LA CARRIERE VIVIER Road, establishing posts at the Northern end of each of these rides.
(b). A. and C.Coys 2nd Roy Mun Fus will advance to G.3.a.8.5. arriving there at Zero plus 100 minutes, where they will be met by 4 Tanks. They will then proceed to Mop up the area as shewn on Coy Commdrs Maps.
A.Coy 2nd Roy Mun Fus will mop up East of the track running from A.26.b.3.9. to A.27.a.8.1. C.Coy 2nd Roy Mun Fus will mop up West of the above track. On completion of mopping up the Battalion will reform and concentrate about A.28.c.8.7. and come into Brigade Reserve.

3. **BARRAGES.**
(a). The H.E.Barrage will be as follows :-- The Left of the 150th Inf Bde will be protected by an enfilade barrage of 18 Pounders and 4.5 Howitzers firing a proportion of smoke. This barrage will come down on the line A.26.b.9.5. to A.27.b.5.3. and will stand until Zero plus 120 minutes, when it will begin to creep Northwards in front of A. and C.Coys.
A Machine Gun barrage will sweep the LEQUESNOY-LANDRECIES Road, and both sides of it from Zero to Zero plus 6 minutes and afterwards will sweep the wood round the Quarries from Zero to Zero plus 60 minutes.
(b). No troops or Tanks will enter the triangle formed by the Red dotted line - the Brigade boundary and the LAIE DE LA CARRIERE VIVIER Road befor Zero plus 150 minutes as it will be bombarded up to that time.
(c). The Barrage covering advance of 2nd Roy Mun Fus will creep to the Left Brigade boundary, arriving there at Zero plus 162 minutes, where it will meet a creeping barrage (coming S.E.) of the 18th Division.

4. **LIAISON POST.**
Will be found by A.Coy 2nd Roy Mun Fusilrs at A.21.d.4.8. to keep touch with the Essex and the Bedford Regts. (18th Division).
18th Division are advancing in a Southerly direction.

5. **INSTRUCTIONS.**
(1). B.Coy 2nd Roy Mun Fus will get in touch with 2nd Northd Fus this afternoon after arrival in Bivouac area. They will proceed independently of the 2nd Roy Mun Fus, with 2nd Northd Fus up to jumping off position digging in in rear of the 2nd Northd Fus.
(2). A. and C.Coys 2nd Roy Mun Fus will dig in South of the BOUSSIES - FONTAINE Road about L.5.d. and L.6.c. moving off from Bivouac area so as to be in position at Zero minus 120 minutes.
(3) Battn Hd/Qrs. will be about L.6.d.5.2. at Zero minus 120 minutes. Advance Battn Hd.Qrs.will be established in Sunken Road at G.3.a. at Zero plus 60 minutes.
(4.) Coys will carry 2 Grenades per man at the rate of 2.NO.23.Grenades to 1.of No.27.
(5.) **SHOVELS.** (a). A. and C.Coys 2nd Roy Mun Fus - each man will carry 1. shovel from POMMEREUIL to neighbourhood of FONTAINE. After digging in these shovels may be stacked and left on the edge of the road to be collected by Regtl Transport later on.
(b). B.Coy 2nd Roy Mun Fus will take 1 shovel per man on the man up to final position mentioned in para 2(a).

6. **LEWIS GUNS.**
Will be carried and proportion of Magazines, as decided on by Coy Comdrs.

7. **GROUND FLARES.**
Will be carried at the rate of 1 per two men and will be lit if called for by contact Aeroplanes.

8. **RATIONS.**
(a). The Breakfast Ration will be cooked and taken on the man when leaving POMMEREUIL.

8. RATIONS.
(b). The remainder of the Rations will be left on Cookers and taken up later in the day as opportunity occurs.
(c). If possible Tea will be issued to night at Bivouac area before moving off.

9. WATER.
(a). Filled Water Carts will be at Bivouac area to night, so that men may start from POMMEREUIL with filled Water Bottles.
(b) Horse Troughs and Water points will be established in Quarry at A.27.d.3.5. and A.27.d.1.7. A 36 feet canvas trough has been erected at L.25.a.2.2.

10. MEDICAL.
Brigade Aid Post will be established under M.O.1/c.2nd Northd Fus in neighbourhood of Bde Hd.Qrs.(G.1.d.2.2).
Advance Dressing Station at L.11.c.3.2.

11. TRANSPORT.
The Regimental Transport will be prepared to move forward to neighbourhood of FONTAINE after 1200 hrs on 4th instant.

12. COMMUNICATIONS.
Coys will notify Battn Hd.Qrs.as soon as they move according to para 5.(1)&(2), and also when they have taken up positions therein mentioned.

13. A C K N O W L E D G E.

xxxxxxxxxxxxxxxxxxxxxxxxxxxxxxxxxxxxxxxxxxxxxxxxxxxxxxxxxxxxxxxxxxxxxx

Issued at .... hrs.

H R Holt   C A P T A I N.

A/ADJUTANT 2ND BATTALION THE ROYAL MUNSTER FUSILIERS.

Copies to :—
No.1. C.O.
  2. Adjut.
  3. H.Q.Coy.
  4. A.Coy.
  5. B.Coy.
  6. C.Coy.
  7. T/Officer.
  8. Qr.Master.
  9. R.S.Major.

D

SECRET.
Copy No.

150TH INFANTRY BRIGADE OPERATION ORDER NO. 208.

1. In continuation of Operation Order No.207 the advance of the 150th Infantry Brigade will be continued to-morrow 8th as laid down therein to the final objective (see attached Map).
Line held by 7th Bn. Wiltshire Regiment is O.25.c.8.8. up line of stream to RENAULT'S BOX 12 inclusive.

2. (a). 7th Bn. Wiltshire Regiment will make good a bridgehead at O.25.d.5.0. forthwith.

   (b) Units will reach HTE NOYELLES as under :-

UNIT.	STARTING POINT.	TIME.	TO	ROUTE.
2nd Bn. R. Munster Fus. 1 Section R.F.A. & 1 Section M.G.C.	Road junction N.5.c.0.7.	06.00 hrs.	HTE NOYELLES.	BASSE NOYELLES RUE DU GRAND MARAIS.
2nd Bn. 15th KRR North'd. Fus.	do.	06.15 hrs.	do.	do.

   (c) Units will be responsible for their own protection East of BASSE NOYELLES

3. As Advances Battalions will advance to the final objective; main bodies checking on the LE CATEAUX PETIT LANDRECIES ROAD until the 2nd Bn. R.Munster Fus. are in touch with the Right Battalion 149th Inf.Brigade but pushing on advance guards beyond. Touch will be maintained between the 2nd Bn. North'd. Fus. and 25th Divn. in so far as this does not check the advance. Beyond this point posts will be dropped along the Divisional boundary to secure the right flank.
   2nd Bn. Royal Munster Fus. from HTE NOYELLES will reach the LE CATEAUX PETIT LANDRECIES ROAD via CHLEM ST. ROCH to cross roads O.21.a.1.7. to O.21.b.15.30.
   2nd Bn. North'd. Fus. via HTE NOYELLES LE CATEAUX Road to point O.27.a.5.0. thence East across country.

4. The 2nd Bn. North'd. Fus. and the 2nd Bn. R.Munster Fus. will each have one section (2 guns) R.F.A. attached to them for these operations. Officers Commanding sections will report to Battalion Headquarters to-night.

5. 7th Bn. Wiltshire Regt. will come into reserve from 07.15. hrs and will move via HTE NOYELLES CHLEM ST.ROCH to MONT DU DIABLE crossing the bridge in O.25.d. in rear of the 150th Inf. Brigade.

6. Brigade Headquarters line of advance will be RUE DES JUIFS - NOYELLES -CHLEM ST.ROCH - MONT DU DIABLE. Advanced Brigade Headquarters will be established at X Roads North of bridge (25.d.) at 07.15.hrs.

7. ACKNOWLEDGE.

Issued at 22.30.hrs.
Thro' Signals.

Captain,
A/Brigade Major.
150th Inf. Brigade.

B

SECRET.
Copy No. 9

150TH INFANTRY BRIGADE ADMINISTRATIVE INSTRUCTIONS No.205.

Reference Maps 57a and 57b (1/40,000).

1. **MEDICAL.** (a) Aid Posts. Battalions will arrange R.A.P's under the M.O's orderly near Battalion Headquarters. Capt. J.F.C. HASLAM, M.C., M.O. i/c 2nd Bn. R. Munster Fusiliers will accompany that Unit; Capt. J. HUNTER, M.O. i/c 2nd Bn. North'd Fusiliers, will select and establish a central Brigade Aid Post in the neighbourhood of Brigade Headquarters and will notify Brigade Headquarters of its exact position; Capt. Z.A. GREEN, M.O. i/c 7th Bn. Wiltshire Regt. will remain at the Transport Lines. Stretcher cases will normally be sent back direct from front line to the Brigade Aid Post, walking and slight cases being given first aid by the M.O.s orderly at R.A.P.

Advanced Dressing Station at L.11.c.3.2.
Large Car Relay Post and Bearer Reserve Post at Farm L.25.a.2.5.

(b) Sick from Battle Surplus and Transport Lines will be sent to 2/2nd.(Nbn) Field Ambulance at K.34.c.7.0.

2. **SUPPLIES.** Normal. No.3 Coy., 50th Divnl. Train has been ordered to be prepared to move forward to L.25.a.5.8. on "Z" day after refilling. Units will issue their own orders as to rations, cookers, etc; attention is drawn to this Office No. A.Q.1762 dated 27th October, 1918.

3. **TRANSPORT.** (a) Regimental Transport will be prepared to move forward to neighbourhood of FONTAINE after 1200 on "Z" day.

(b) 1 limber and 2 pack animals per Battalion will be detailed for ammunition supply as laid down in para. 5. The limbers will be under the command of N.C.O. to be detailed by 7th Bn. Wiltshire and will arrive at neighbourhood of L.13.b.5.0. at Zero hour on "Z" day. The N.C.O. will immediately get into touch with Brigade Headquarters. The pack animals will be under the command of a N.C.O. to be detailed by 2nd Bn. R. Munster Fusiliers and will arrive at neighbourhood of G.7.c. central at Zero + 1 hours on "Z" day; the N.C.O. will at once get into touch with Brigade Headquarters.

4. **WATER.** Horse troughs and water points will be established in Quarry at A.27.d.3.5. and A.27.d.1.7. A 36-ft canvas trough has been erected at L.25.a.2.2.

5. **S.A.A., GRENADES, ETC.** (i) A Divisional dump of S.A.A. (bundle packed and clip), Grenades (Nos. 23, 27 and 34), S.O.S. (limited quantity only), V.P.A. 1" white, Red Ground Flares and 3" Stokes Shells, will be established at L.17.a.2.1.

Demands for S.A.A., etc., will be sent to Brigade Headquarters, who will make arrangements to send requirements forward.

If necessary, a Brigade dump will be formed under the orders of Brigade Headquarters, ammunition being sent forward by pack animals; and the dump replenished by limbers from the Divisional dump.

(ii) 3" Stokes shells will be taken forward by 150th Trench Mortar Battery in its own limbers as far as possible and will be carried the remaining distance under arrangements made by O.C. 150th Trench Mortar Battery. Any shells required in replacement will be demanded as above and transport sent to Brigade Headquarters.

P.T.O.

Sheet No.2.

(iii) Demands for S.O.S. rockets must be kept low; there is a tendency to demand an excessive quantity, and it appears that the infrequency of their use is sometimes overlooked.

6. ORDNANCE. (i) D.A.D.O.S. will be prepared to issue Lewis Guns and components in replacement from dump at L.17.a.2.1. at Zero + 3 hours. Demands will be sent to Brigade Headquarters, who will arrange for guns, etc. to be sent up. Lewis Guns for repair can be sent down to this dump.

(ii) Units will demand stores to replace deficiencies as soon as possible after the battle, a list of the important items being sent to Rear Brigade Headquarters. Arrangements are being made for web equipment, etc. to be collected and handed over to D.A.D.O.S., and advantage should be taken of all salvage to replace deficiencies. A covering indent is not required for Lewis Guns sent up under para. 6 (i).

7. VETERINARY. An Advanced Veterinary Post will be established at K.30.b.9.2. at Zero + 3 hours.

8. STRAGGLERS. Stragglers collecting posts will be established at L.4.d.0.2., L.11.c.5.2. and L.17.a.8.5. Soup kitchens will be established at these points by O. i/c Divisional Canteen. These posts will be pushed forward as the situation demands.

9. PRISONERS OF WAR CAGE at L.8.d.9.2., whither prisoners will be sent under Battalion escorts.

10 BURIALS will be arranged by Divisional Burials Officer. It is the business of everyone to remove any dead which may be lying on roads or tracks, and place them adjacent to such roadways and out of the way of traffic, where they will be collected in due course by Divisional Burial Party. Orders will be issued to all ranks that no identification discs or personal effects of any kind are to be removed from the dead except by a duly authorised burial party.

11. BATTLE SURPLUS. Battle Surplus will be prepared to move to new area in or near LE CATEAU before 1500 tomorrow.

12. LOCATIONS.
    (a) Divisional Headquarters - LE FAYT FARM.
    (b) Rear Divnl. Headquarters - LE CATEAU.
    (c) Brigade Headquarters - L.6.q.3.3.
    (d) Rear Brigade Headquarters - present location in LE CATEAU.

13. CASUALTIES. Endeavours must be made to send early estimates of casualties; in previous battles these estimates have been received very late in some cases.

14. DIVISIONAL CANTEEN. The Divisional Canteen is now open in the Shop at K.34.d.30.45.

Issued at 2130 hours, through Signals

Captain,
Staff Captain,
150th Infantry Brigade

Copy No. 1. G.O.C.
2. Bde. Major.
3. Staff Captain.
4. 2nd North'd Fus.
5. do.
6. 7th Wilts. Regt.
7. do.
8. 2nd R. Munster Fus.
9. do. Rear.

10. 150th Trench Mortar Bty.
11. M.O.i/c 2nd North'd Fus.
12. M.O.i/c 7th Wilts Regt.
13. M.O.i/c 2nd R. Muns. Fus.
Rear.14. No.5 Coy., A.S.C.
15. A.D.M.S.
Rear.16. 1/1st (Nbn) Field Ambce.
17. War Diary.
18. File.

SECRET

B.M.802.
8-11-18.

G.O.C.
2nd Bn. North'd Fusiliers.
7th Bn. Wiltshire Regt.
2nd Bn. R. Munster Fusiliers.
150th Trench Mortar Battery.

WARNING ORDER No. B.M. 802.

From information it appears that the enemy will retire swiftly tomorrow. 150th Infantry Brigade will be Mobile Brigade for pursuit and will be ready to move at ½ hrs notice from 0700 hours tomorrow. Officers Commanding Battalions and Trench Mortar Battery will take steps to ensure that all horses are shod up to date, men's boots are in good repair and in good condition and that all kits and transport is lightened as much as possible.

Acknowledge

Headquarters,
150th Infantry Brigade.
8th November, 1918.

Captain,
Brigade Major,
150th Infantry Brigade.

COPY.

B.M. 101.
9/11/18.

O.C.
2nd Bn. Northd. Fusiliers.
7th Bn. Wiltshire Regiment.
2nd Bn. The Royal Munster Fusiliers.
150th Trench Mortar Battery.

The Brigadier General Commanding wishes to congratulate all ranks on the magnificent work they performed during the last six weeks.

They have fought successfully without exception, the Brigade never having failed to carry out the task set it, undergoing on many occasions great hardships without the slightest complaint.

The Brigadier has hoped that the Brigade would have been allowed to still closely follow the Boshe whom it has so often defeated.

However, the Brigade have the satisfaction that it has advanced further than any other Allied soldiers and has driven the Boshe out of Northern France on its front.

(signed) GEO. ROLLS

HEADQUARTERS,
150TH INFANTRY BRIGADE,   BRIGADIER GENERAL,
9TH NOVEMBER 1918.   150TH INFANTRY BRIGADE.

COPY.

MAJOR GENERAL JACKSON, COMMANDING 50TH
DIVISION, WISHES ALL RANKS TO KNOW HE
IS VERY PLEASED INDEED WITH THE ADVANCE
OF THE BRIGADE TODAY. B.G.C. WISHES
TO ADD HIS CONGRATULATIONS TO THOSE OF
THE MAJOR GENERAL COMMANDING.

SECRET.   Copy No. 3

150TH INFANTRY BRIGADE OPERATION ORDER NO.205.

Ref.Map.57a. 1/40,000.

1. The 2nd Bn. R.Munster Fusiliers will be clear of their present area in LE CATEAU by 1400 hours 3rd November.

2. They will move to an area about L.19.b.&.d. to be reconnoitred in conjunction with the 2nd Bn. North'd. Fusiliers to-day.

3. Arrival in new area will be reported to this Office.

4. ACKNOWLEDGE.

Issued at   hours.
Thro' Signals.

Captain,
A/Brigade Major.
150th Inf.Brigade.

Copy No. 1. 50th Division.
        2. 149th Inf.Brigade.
        3. 2nd Bn. R.Munster Fusiliers.
        4. 2nd Bn. North'd. Fusiliers.
        5. War Diary.
        6. File.

WAR DIARY 2nd Royal Munster Fusiliers
INTELLIGENCE SUMMARY
Army Form C. 2118.

December 1918

Place	Date	Hour	Summary of Events and Information	Remarks and references to Appendices
TINQUEROS	1/12/18		Strength of Battn. 39 Officers 806 Other Ranks (incl. attached)	
"	2/12/18		2/Lt J.R. Boyd. M.M. The Connaught Rangers joined Bn. for duty. 2/Lt R. Coulter The Connaught Rangers joined the Bn for duty. Routine parades etc.	A.2.3 / A.2.1K
"	3/12/18	1000	Bn. paraded in strong in parade to proceed to Euvrenade 1000 yds E. of DOMPIERRE Station to meet H.M. The King. Bn. paraded 34 Officers 375 O.R. Battn. arrived first on scene to receive his majesty. Major Williams M.C. — the Commanding Officer — had the honour of being received by H.M. the King who kindly sent actual after the Strength of the Battn. and Progress of "Education Scheme". Lieut D. Hickey rejoined Battn.	A
"	4/12/18		Lieut I.T. Shefield & 3 O.R. proceeded to WARDRUES-LES-GRAND to take over the duties of Area Commandant. 2/Lt Friedman 1 Sergt and 3 O.R. proceeded on similar duty to AMAND-ST-LIEU.	H.2.K
"		1100	36 O.R. from hotel in Camp. Auditional Joined Battn.	Sub.

Army Form C. 2118.

WAR DIARY
or
INTELLIGENCE SUMMARY. 2nd Royal Munster Fusiliers
Sheet 1
(Erase heading not required.)

Instructions regarding War Diaries and Intelligence Summaries are contained in F. S. Regs., Part II. and the Staff Manual respectively. Title pages will be prepared in manuscript.

Place	Date	Hour	Summary of Events and Information	Remarks and references to Appendices
Solesmes	14/12/18		Companies at the disposal of Comp. Commanders during the morning for Kit Inspection &c. Battn. route marching Coys at 1400 hrs. Lieutenant Major Williams awarded D.S.O/Sergt. Livingston the M.C. 2nd Lieut W.J. Mayurn awarded M.C.	App A
"	15/12/18			
"	16/12/18		Routine parades	App A
"	17/12/18		Battn paraded 0755 & moved to LE QUESNOY. Colour party with Kings + Regimental Colours rejoined the Battn.	"B"
LE QUESNOY	18/12/18		Parade 0845 - Battn. marched to ETH & went into billets. Major C.R. Williams D.S.O. M.C. assumed command of the Battn. H.Q. situated in ETH Chateau. Front of billets very bad owing to heavy fighting early in November	App A
ETH	19/12/18	1600	Coys cleaning billets in morning. "B" Coy Strength 2 Offrs + 120 OR moved over to the village of BRY on account of bad condition of billets	App B

Army Form C. 2118.

WAR DIARY
INTELLIGENCE SUMMARY.

(Erase heading not required.)

Dec 1918
Sheet IV
2/R.M.F.

Place	Date	Hour	Summary of Events and Information	Remarks and references to Appendices
ETH	20/12/18		Coys cleaning billeting area.	AAA
"	21/12/18		Coys cleaning up billets. Bn. S.B's mess started in the Chateau. A draft 15 OR joined	AAA
"	22/12/18		Church Parades in the morning. Draft 6 OR joined Bath. Lieut E. McCarthy U.S.M.C. joined Battn as M.O.	AAA
"	23/12/18		Cleaning Kits & wash to during the day. Xmas Criosmais drill in morning. 2/Lt E.F. Hickey RDF joined for Bn.	AAA
"	24/12/18		Routine work. 30 OR (nurses) to proceed to steamships as miners. 235/ midnight mass at Bdg.	
"	25/12/18		Xmas day. Owing to unfortunate circumstances Xmas dinner & other usual festivities could not be held.	AAA
"	26/12/18		Routine Parades. 10 OR despatched to CAMBRAI to be demobilized as miners. Concert in evening in "D" Coy dining hall	AAA
"	27/12/18	0900-1200	Coys employed on Salvage. Class for Regular & Special Reserve Officers commenced under Lt Col Hardman Jones 2/Northumberland Fus.	

WAR DIARY
INTELLIGENCE SUMMARY

Army Form C. 2118

2/Royal Munster Fusiliers

Dec. 1918 Sheet 1

Place	Date	Hour	Summary of Events and Information	Remarks and references to Appendices
TAISNIÈRES	5/12/18		Major Williams late of 3rd R.S.M. Ricey & 14 O.R's proceeded to England to being [being] reabs. Regimental Colours. Lecture by Ord Survey [?] Instructor on Reinforce Drafts. 2/Lt. McCay M.M.	
"	6/12/18		2/Lt. McCay arrived with a draft of 31 men of Bn newly drafted for Special Service. Battalion Route March at 0930 hrs to 1230 hrs. 2/Lt F. Parsell admitted [to] hospital	
"	7/12/18		Routine Parades. Baths &c. Billeting Officer went to inspect on the 4th area.	
"	8/12/18		Church Parades at Taisnières. 2/Lt. Lowndes reported from base Batt.	
"	9/12/18		Parade's under Company Commanders. 2/Lts B.J. Thomas & Obut? reported from Base.	
"	10/12/18		Batt. parades as strong as possible to practice "ceremonial parade" for presentation of medals. Batt. Officers 42 O.R. 949	
"	11/12/18		Batt. Route march via Monceau & Saurd. Weather very bad. 2/Lt Lowndes reported off leave. Draft of 33 O.R's reported from U.K.	
"	12/12/18		Another ceremonial parade for presentation of medals. 2/Lts Dubois & Burgess proceeded on leave to Brussels	
"	13/12/18		Presentation of medals postponed owing to bad weather. Bn were under Company arrangements. Batn Strength Off. 41 O.R. 402	

Army Form C. 2118.

WAR DIARY
or
INTELLIGENCE SUMMARY.
(Erase heading not required.)

Dec 1918
2/R.M.F.
Sheet 5

Place	Date	Hour	Summary of Events and Information	Remarks and references to Appendices
ETH	28/12		Wet day. Coys unable to continue Salvage work	11/2/1
"	29/12		Sunday. Usual Divine Service Parades.	12/2/2
"	30/12		Coys employed on Salvage work in morning	13/2/2
"	31/12		Coys employed on Salvage work in morning	
			Major R.N. Purdon MC 4th R.M.F. rejoined Battn from Senior	14/2/4
			Officers Course Aldershot	

Moorhouse Major
Cmdg 2/Royal Munster Fusiliers

29 January 1919

WAR DIARY 2/Royal Munster Fusiliers

INTELLIGENCE SUMMARY

Army Form C. 2118.

Sheet 1

Place	Date	Hour	Summary of Events and Information	Remarks and references to Appendices
ETH	1/1/19		Fine day - Men had their Christmas dinners which arrived during the week	A/2/24
"	2/1/19		Fine day. Coys employed on salvage work in morning - 20 men of A Coy placed in isolation owing to a case of measles amongst civilians of BRY. The Batt. Isolated party moved to BRY.	A/2/24
	3/1/19		Routine parade & salvage work.	A/2/24
	4/1/19		Routine parade & salvage work	A/2/24
	5/1/19		Wed Day 15th + 7 OR sent to base for disposal on demobilisation (Lt Col. Hillyard)	A/2/24 A/2/24
"	6/1/19	0900	R.C. Church parade (BRY Church). Ceremonial parade in morning	A/2/24
	7/1/19		Ceremonial parade followed by salvage work - Coy football competition	A/2/24
			"C" beat "B" in morning - "D" beat "A" in afternoon.	
	8/1/19	1430	GOC 58th Div (Maj Gen Jackson DSO) presented immediate Awards to:- Major C.R. Williams M.C. (DSO) Capt. H.S. Hobb (MC) 20383 Pte J.E. Kent (DCM) 8576 CSM Murphy MM. 8522 L/C P Murphy MM (both bar to MM) 5371 Pte Bentley	"A"
			8243 Cpl Gallagher 2607 Pte Lawrence 5994 Pte Bragg 3625 Sgt Hullinger	
"			20126 Sgt Greenwood, 20054 Pte Beaton 20032 Cpl Fox 20084 Cpl Webb 5337 Pte Mann	A/2/24
			The above were awarded by Lt Gen L Rothwell + 27 M Clean MM	

Army Form C. 2118.

WAR DIARY
or
INTELLIGENCE SUMMARY.

2/R-M-F-

(Erase heading not required.)

Instructions regarding War Diaries and Intelligence Summaries are contained in F. S. Regs., Part II. and the Staff Manual respectively. Title pages will be prepared in manuscript.

Jan 1919. Sheet 11

Place	Date	Hour	Summary of Events and Information	Remarks and references to Appendices
E.T.H	9/1/19		2 Lorries sent to help Bath in Salvage work.	17/1/18
	10/1/19		Coys employed in morning on Salvage work. 2/Lt. Hayes & 11 OR reported to unit from 150 T.M.B.y also 2/Lt. McGuire Connaught Rangers and 1 OR reported from 150 T.M. Batty but the men attached to OO XIII Corps. 18 OR reported from base	A/25
"	11/1/19		Salvage work in morning. Bn Cross Country Run in afternoon. Order of Coys "D" 22 pts "C" 21 pts "B" 14 pts "A" 10 points	A/26
"	12/1/19		Usual Divine Service Parades	A/24
"	13/1/19		Salvage work in morning.	A/26
"	14/1/19		Salvage work in morning. Baron & Baroness Estreux etc. of E.T.H Chateau (Bn H.Q) came to visit their property & lunched with Bn. 4/9 Miss Bruce with agreement [?] & 13 OR [?]	A/26
"	15/1/19		Have hunt in the morning, football match with agreement [?] Scotch in the morning. The Army Pony Camic [?]	A/26
"	16/1/19		Salvage work in the morning. Party gave a concert in "D" Coys dining hall at 19.30	A/26
"	17/1/19		Salvage work run the morning - afternoon - games	A/26

WAR DIARY 2nd Bn The Royal Munster Fusiliers or INTELLIGENCE SUMMARY

Army Form C. 2118.

January 1919   Sheet III

Place	Date	Hour	Summary of Events and Information	Remarks and references to Appendices
BTH	18/1/19		Arms Drill 0900 to 0930. Remainder of the morning Salvage work	field
	19/1/19		Usual Divine Service Parade – Afternoon Semi-Final of Divisional football Competition 2/2nd N.F.A. v WAR GAMES – LE –	
	20/1/19		GRAND – (Result NILS 3 goals – 2/2nd N F A 2 goals) Routine parades and Salvage work – IICorps Cross Country Run. 17 to U.K. off for demobilisation "B" field	field
"	21/1/19		Routine parades and Salvage work – Afternoon Capt MORSE lectures to the Battalion in "D" Coy's Dining Hall on "Demobilisation"	field
"	22/1/19		Drill 0900 – 0930 – followed by Hare Hunt, caught 2 hare and 3 picked up. Afternoon football match "A" v "B" Coy Baron Corps (Result – a draw)	field
"	23/1/19		Very frosty – Routine Parades – Afternoon "A" Coy move to CURGIES –	field
"	24/1/19		"B" & "C" Coys move to CURGIES – Afternoon Hockey match 2nd R.M.F. v Representative 149th Infantry Brigade – Result 2nd R.M.F 6 goals – 149 Inf Bde Nil	field
"	25/1/19		Bn HQ the QM and "D" Coy move to CURGIES – 3/Lieuts Murphy Loutor + 25 O.R's U.K. for demobilisation	field
CURGIES	26/1/19		Slight fall of snow – Usual Divine Service parades	field
"	27/1/19		Snowy – Routine Parades – Afternoon Bty Hdqrs Coy Commrs mtg	field
"	28/1/19		Snowy – Routine parades – Route march	field

January 1919 - Sheet IV

WAR DIARY 2nd Bn. Royal Munster Fusiliers

INTELLIGENCE SUMMARY. Army Form C. 2118.

Place	Date	Hour	Summary of Events and Information	Remarks and references to Appendices
CURGIES	29/1/19		Routine Parades -	
"	30/1/19		Routine Parades -	
"	31/1/19		Very frosty - Routine Parades -	
	31/1/19			

Comdg. 2nd Bn. Royal Munster Fusiliers

February 1919   Sheet I   WAR DIARY 2nd Bn. Royal Munster Fusiliers   Army Form C. 2118.

INTELLIGENCE SUMMARY.
(Erase heading not required.)

Place	Date	Hour	Summary of Events and Information	Remarks and references to Appendices
CURGIES	1/2/19		Very frosty. Routine Parade — 35 O'Ranks despatched to base for despersal to U.K. for demobilization.	
"	2/2/19		Usual Divine Service Parade.	fivt.R.
"	3-2-19		Routine Parade —	fivt.R.
"	4-2-19		Route march in the afternoon. 3 lorries reported and took 60 men of the Battn. to the theatre at Valenciennes.	fivt.R.
"	5-2-19		Very frosty. Routine Parade —	fivt.R.
"	6-2-19		Very severe frost. Routine Parade —	fivt.R.
"	7-2-19		Frosty. Routine Parade — 40 O.R. despatched to base for despersal to U.K. for demobilization.	fivt.R.
"	8-2-19		Severe frost. Routine Parade — 2 Officers and 44 O.R. also despatched to base for despersal to U.K. for demobilization (2/Lieuts Howell & Gilpin) M.O. Ranks despatched to base.	fivt.R.
"	9-2-19		Usual Divine service parade — for despersal to U.K. for demobilization. Afternoon "B" Coy football team played no 3 Coy. A.S.C. at PREUX-AU-SART (Result 2 goals, 1 to 4 goals)	fivt.R.
"	10-2-19		Frosty weather. Route March.	fivt.R.
"	11-2-19		Very severe frost. Battn. re-organized and formed in to two ?	fivt.R.

WAR DIARY or INTELLIGENCE SUMMARY

Army Form C. 2118.

February 1919 Sheet II 2nd Battn. Royal Munster Fusiliers

Place	Date	Hour	Summary of Events and Information	Remarks and references to Appendices
CURGIES	11-2-19		Company trains - Capt. W.B. Webb M.C. appointed from 11.O.R. command same 9/2/19	
"	12.2.19		Frosty weather. 31 O.R. despatched to 50 Div. Reception Camps for disposal on demobilization	
"	13.2.19		Sunny day. 11 O.R. sent away for disposal	
"	14.2.19		Rain in morning. Frost broken. 9 O.R. sent away for disposal	
"	15.2.19		Thaw continued. G.O.C. 50th Div inspected details of 7th R. Munsh. F's. 3 O.R. to U.K. on disposal. Maj. R.H.Parsons 4/12 M.F. appointed act. Lt. Col.	
"	16.2.19		Usual divine service parade. 6 O.R. sent away on disposal	
"	17.2.19		2nd Lt. L. Rathorne sent to U.K. for 2 months leave pending information of unit for European Forces. 1st Lieut E. McCarthy U.S.M.C. left B'n on reporting to H.Q. 2 C.C.S. Gr. Rds left 150 1030.	
"	18.2.19		Coys employed on salvage work & at education classes	
"	19.2.19		Battn. out in morning on a Route March - S.E. of Curgies. Capt. T. Nevin M.C. to O.R.	
"	20.2.19		Coys employed in salvage & Education in morning. Left Battn for disposal	
"	21.2.15		2/Lt. E.F. Hickey R. Dublin Fus. - Left Battn to join 1st R. Dublin Fusiliers. 23 O.R. proceeded (under 2/Lt D.Swift) for disposal.	

WAR DIARY

February 1919   2/ Royal Munster Fusiliers   Sheet III

INTELLIGENCE SUMMARY

Army Form C. 2118.

Place	Date	Hour	Summary of Events and Information	Remarks and references to Appendices
CURGIES	22/2/19		Wet morning. Got 150 Bde. inspected Bath, Cibili dhoing the morning.	initials
"	23/2/19		No C. of E. Church parade. R.E. parade 11.05 hrs. 3. O.R. disposed.	initials
	24/2/19		Coys employed on Salvage in morning. Several officers & men proceeded to MARLY in morning to witness final of 1st Army Tug o'War. 6th weights in which 1st R.M.F. were pulling. In afternoon Capt.	
"	25/2/19		J.F. Shea R.S.M. O'Callaghan M.C. D.C.M. and 2 O.R. of 1st RMF visited the Bath. Major C.R. Williams ask me permitted to remain at home on 2 months leave pending reforming of Bath, for foreign service. This was the first occasion since Lucknow that the C.O. of 1st & this Battn established the two Batt. Sgt Majors together.	initials
"	26th		5 O.R. proceeded to base for disposal. Batn employment usual Salvage work in morning.	initials
	27th		Coys employed on Salvage and Education in morning	initials

WAR DIARY

2nd Royal Munster Fusiliers

Army Form C. 2118.

Sheet IV

INTELLIGENCE SUMMARY.

(Erase heading not required.)

February 1919

Place	Date	Hour	Summary of Events and Information	Remarks and references to Appendices
CURGIES	28		45 Ors 42 OR proceeded to Boulogne to join 1st Regiment	
			Irish Rgt. AIF	
			3 OR. proceeded to Caen on dispersal	MSS
			Ru? morning — Chaplain to be proceeded with adjutant to Amiens to bring back portable altar belonging to Bn which was left in the care of Sister of Charity Amiens in May 1917	MSS
	28th		Strength of Battn.	
			34 Offrs. 316 OR. 40 Animals	
Curgies (Nr Valenciennes) France.				

M.H. Anderson Lt Col
C in of 2/Royal Munster Fusiliers

Army Form C. 2118.

WAR DIARY
or
INTELLIGENCE SUMMARY.

2/Royal Munster Fusiliers   March 1919   Sheet 1

(Erase heading not required.)

Place	Date	Hour	Summary of Events and Information	Remarks and references to Appendices
Curgie	1st		Revd honorary Capt Roth & Capt Mahrin returned from Amiens with kits & etc after the property of the Bn. which had been deposited there in safe custody since May 1917. 2/Lt B. Boyd MM (The Connaught Rangers), 2/Lt N. Cash, 2/Lt R. Armstrong MM (R. Sub. Fus), 2/Lt E.T. Burgess & 42 OR proceeded to Bourboure on reporting to 7th R. Irish Regt. Capt. C. Tennant and 41 OR proceed to Receving Camp for dispersal — Summer Time came into force at 1300 hrs (i.e. Clocks were advanced to 2400).	App A
Curgie	2nd	1130	CO at a Conference at 150 Bde. — Usual Church parades	App A
Wargnies-le-Petit	3rd	1300	Battn moved to Wargnies-le-Petit. Rained all the way during march of two hours.	App A
"	4th		Battn. rearranged into one Company Capt Gloster M.C. O.C. employed in cleaning billeting area.	App B
"	5th	0830	All available men sent to Curgies for Salvage work, returning 1615	App C

Army Form C. 2118.

2/Royal Munster Fusiliers

WAR DIARY
or
INTELLIGENCE SUMMARY.

Sheet 1   March 1919.

(Erase heading not required.)

Instructions regarding War Diaries and Intelligence Summaries are contained in F. S. Regs., Part II. and the Staff Manual respectively. Title pages will be prepared in manuscript.

Place	Date	Hour	Summary of Events and Information	Remarks and references to Appendices
Wagnies- le-Petit	6th	0900	All available men sent to Angies for Salvage. Books returning 1800	
"	7		2/Lt A.F. Duke proceeded to U.K. for Course at Trinity College Oxford and Struck off strength of Bn. 10 O.R. sent to Div. Reception Camp for disposal.	1924
"			Men not sent out on Salvage on account of their having just met the firing obsy. C.O's 1st inspection in morning. 24 O.R. to Div. Reception Camp for disposal.	18/24
"	8		wet day. 26 O.R. proceeded to Div. Reception Camp on disposal	16/24
"	9		Usual divine service parade.	15/24
"	10		Cleaning Lewis guns &c.	11/24
"	11		All available men employed on Salvage.	14/24
"	12		22 O.R. proceeded to Div. Reception Camp on disposal. 0900 - 1500 (New CVO & 159) 2/Lt Majnck struck 5/7 strength on discharge from S. for steps after sentence by G.C.M. to be dismissed H.M. Service.	17/24
"	13		2/Lt. T.H. Groom & 2/Lt. M. Clair MM struck off strength of Bn. on reporting to Prisoner of War Corps. All available men employed on Salvage in morning.	14/24

A6945 Wt. W14422/M160 135,000 12/16 D. D. & L. Forms/C/2118/14.

Army Form C. 2118.

WAR DIARY
or
INTELLIGENCE SUMMARY.
(Erase heading not required.)

2/1 Royal Munster Fusiliers   Sheet III   March 1919

Place	Date	Hour	Summary of Events and Information	Remarks and references to Appendices
Wagnies-le-Petit	14th		Warning order received by wire (150586 S.S.6.6) That Ryder units for foreign service will commence entraining for U.K. on 16th inst. proceeding as Cadre "A"	A.3.1
"	15th		Capt. A.G. Dumpleton M.C. Lieut M.B. Slevin + Lieut Rev D. Searcy proceed to Reception Camp for dispersal + thence of thenith	A.3.2
"	16th	10.30	O.C. at Le Quesnoy to meet Field Marshall C-in-C.	
			No C.S.O.E. Church parade - Usual R.C. Church parade. 22 O.R. to Reception Camp for dispersal. Orders to move of cadre cancelled	A.3.3 A.3.4
"	17th	10.00	R.C. parade mass. (St Patrick's Day)	A.3.5
"	18		Usual routine parade	A.3.6
"	19		12 O.R. to Reception Camp for dispersal	A.3.7
"	20		Available men employed under Q.M. on fatigues. Sleet in the morning	A.3.8
"	21		Men employed on cleaning Bn equipment	A.3.9
"	22		All men at baths. Information received that cadre of 2nd Leinster Regt will relieve Bn	A.3.10
"	23		Usual divine service parades	A.3.11
"	24		2/Lt Crowley & 15 O.R. returned from XIII Corps school. 6 O.R. proceeded to East reception camp for dispersal	A.3.12

2/Royal Munster Fusiliers

WAR DIARY
INTELLIGENCE SUMMARY.

Army Form C. 2118.

Wargnies Part IV March 1919

Place	Date	Hour	Summary of Events and Information	Remarks and references to Appendices
Wargnies-le-Petit	25		All available men employed on salvage at 5TH Chateau - 2r Sheffield and 1/R rejoined from duty Area Commandant Wargnies-le-Grand	7.2.D.11
"	26		Cold day - Sleet -	1-4-11
"	27		Lieut. Revd. R. Morrissey C.F. to U.K. on leave	7-3-19
"	28		Inspection of cadre by C.O. 12 L.D. Mules transferred to 50 M.G. Coy.	
"	29		2/Lt Goodman + 30 O.R. rejoined from duty as Area Commandant L156 ST AMAND	17 A.sh
"	30		Snow -	17 1.46
"	31		2 - O.R. to U.K. on leave — 6 O.R. (including smith Cadre R) to Reception Camp for disposal. Fine	
			Strength of Bath at H.Q. 146 Officers 54 O.R. 6 L.D. Mules on command 2 " 6 " —	A-3-19

Wargnies-le-Petit
31/3/19

M.F. Dixon Lieut Col.
Comdg. 2/Royal Munster Fusiliers

RE-ORGANIZATION OF BATTALION.

1....... From March 4th, the Battalion will be Re-organized into ONe Company under Captain.J.F.G.Gloster. M.C.

2....... Each Platoon of above Coy will be composed of men drawn from late "A","B","C", and "D",Coys.
C.S.M. S.Tyrrell,M.M,and C.Q.M.S. W.Howe,M.M,will perform duties of C.S.M.and C.Q.M.S.of this Coy.
C.Q.M.S. A.Windibank will be attached to Hd.Qr.Detachment for duty.

xxxxxxxxxxxxxxxxxxxxxxxxxxxxxxxxxxxxxxxxxxxxxx

H. B. HOLT. Captain.

A/Adjutant 2nd Battalion The Royal Munster Fusiliers

"PART.I."   B A T T A L I O N   O R D E R S.   **"NO. 53."**

BY

LIEUT-COL. B.H. PURDON, M.C. COMMDG 2ND BATTALION THE ROYAL MUNSTER FUSILIERS.

GURGIES.   S U N D A Y.   2nd March, 1919.

1. DETAIL.
Orderly Officer for duty tomorrow :- 2nd Lieut. F.J. Hurley.
In Waiting :- 2nd Lieut. A.F. Duke.

2. RETREAT.
Retreat will until further orders be sounded at 1730 hours.

3. PARADES.
I. The Battalion will move to WARGNIES-LE-PETIT tomorrow. Parade on the Village Square at 1300 hours.

II. Lieut. B.J. Pegum will proceed at 0900 hours with a Billeting party of 3 other ranks to be detailed by each of the Officers Commdg "A" and "B" Coys.
The Battalion will be billeted on the Basis of "Headquarters" and "One Company". (see attached re-organization of Battalion).

III. Dinners will be served at 1200 hours.

IV. ROUTE:- GURGIES - JENLAIN - G.20.central - WARGNIES-LE-PETIT.

V. TRANSPORT:- Limbers as under will be placed at the disposal of O.C. Coys.
(a). Coys will send guides to Orderly Room at 0800 hours to meet these Limbers:-
"A" Coy:- 5 Limbers from 2nd Bn North'd Fusiliers.
"B" Coy:- 5 Limbers from the 7th Wilts Regt.
As soon as loaded these will proceed to WARGNIES-LE-PETIT under orders of O.C. Coys concerned.
Officers Kits, Stoves, Forms, Benches, and Latrine Equipment will be carried by Coys.
(b). At 1000 hours Battalion Limbers will report as follows :-
Orderly Room:- 1.Limber.   Hd.Qr.Mess:- 1.Limber and Mess Cart
Medical Inspection Room:- Maltese Cart.
Remainder of Battalion Transport as arranged by the Qr.Master.

H. B. H O L T. Captain.

A/Adjutant 2nd Battalion The Royal Munster Fusiliers.

2/Royal Munster Fusiliers

Army Form C. 2118.

WAR DIARY or INTELLIGENCE SUMMARY.

(Erase heading not required.)

Sheet 1 — April 1919

Place	Date	Hour	Summary of Events and Information	Remarks and references to Appendices
WARGNIES-LE- PETIT	1st	1100	Drill parade for all available OR. Fine day	staff
"	2nd		Lt Col B.N. Pardon MC proceeded to Paris on leave of absence. Capt Trapp	staff
"	3rd		A/s Hott assumed Command of Bath.	staff
"	"		Information received that Cadre 2nd Munsters expected to arrive shortly for s/mot.	staff
"	4th		Acting ADMS. 50th Div inspected Sanitary arrangements of Bath. 5 officers & 170R.	staff
"	"		Sent by motor lorry to spend afternoon in Valenciennes.	staff
"	5th		All available men employed under Q.M.	staff
"	6th		No C.O.E divine Service parade. Naval R.C. parade. 2 OR. to Div reception Camp — for dispersal.	staff
"	7th	0800	Cadre 2nd Munsters Rgt. arrived. Lt Col B.N. Pardon MC returned from leave of absence & resumed Command of Bath.	staff
"	8th		Bath. equipment handed over on vouchers to 2nd Leinsters Rgt.	staff
"	9th	1100	CO's inspection of Cadre in marching order.	staff
"	10th		2nd Lt. A.F. Duke rejoined from Course of instruction at OXFORD — 2 OR. to Hosp. —	staff
"	11th		In afternoon hockey match between 2/RMF v 2/Leinsters.	staff
"	12		Cold day. 1 OR. to hospital	staff

Army Form C. 2118.

WAR DIARY
or
INTELLIGENCE SUMMARY.
(Erase heading not required.)

2/Royal Munster Fusiliers   Sheet 1   April 1919

Place	Date	Hour	Summary of Events and Information	Remarks and references to Appendices
Wargnies-le-	13th		1 O.R. to Div. Reception Camp for demobilization. 1 O.R. rejoined from Div. W.S.	
Petit	14th		1 O.R. transferred to 7th R. Irish Regt.	
"	15		1 O.R. rejoined from Base as reinforcement - 1 O.R. rejoined from hosp.	
"	16		2 O.R. to No. 11 Prison as escort to Pte (Infty) O'Donnell (5 years P.S.) 1 O.R. from hospital	
"	17		3 O.R. on Command transferred to 7/R. Irish Regt.	
"	18	1400	Good Friday — Army to take all available O.Rs. to Services at the Piggery.	
"	19		1 O.R. rejoined from 50th Div. W.R.	
"	20		2 O.R. transferred to 7th R. Irish Regt. — 2 O.R. to Div. Dispersal Camp.	
"	21		Easter Monday — observed as a holiday — 2/Lt. Purdon M.C. gazetted as Temp. Lt. Col.	
"	22		Lt. Col. Purdon MC proceeded on duty to Base. Capt. & Adjt. Abbott resumed Command of Bn. during his absence	
"	23		Kit parade for all available men under R.Q.M.S. 2/Lt. F.J. Hurley reported for duty	
			under D.A.D.Q.R.F. No. 3 Area	
"	24		1 O.R. from hosp.	
"	25	1030	Medical Inspection of Cadre.	
"	26		Lt. Col. Purdon M.C. resumed Command of Battn. 1 O.R. (Pte Madigan - Ancestry Bn on parade) rejoined from 50th Div. W.R.M.	

Army Form C. 2118.

WAR DIARY
or
INTELLIGENCE SUMMARY.
(Erase heading not required.)

Instructions regarding War Diaries and Intelligence Summaries are contained in F. S. Regs., Part II. and the Staff Manual respectively. Title pages will be prepared in manuscript.

Place	Date	Hour	Summary of Events and Information	Remarks and references to Appendices
Wagnies-le-Petit	27th		Usual Church parade - 1 Offr to Div Reception Camp for dispersal	nil
	28th		1 Offr. to U.K. on leave	AB4
	29th		CO's kit inspection of Battn. - 2nd Horsing Off rejoined from leave	AB4 nil
	30th		Wet day	nil
			Strength Battn. 16 Officers 46 OR.	

Wagnies-le-Petit
30-4-19.

M.P.W. O'Connor Lt Col.
Cmdg 2/Royal Munster Fusiliers

2ND BATTALION,
ROYAL MUNSTER
FUSILIERS.

War Diary

2nd Royal Munster Fusiliers

May 1919

2/ Royal Munster Fusiliers

WAR DIARY
or
INTELLIGENCE SUMMARY

Army Form C. 2118.

Sheet 1.

May 1919

Place	Date	Hour	Summary of Events and Information	Remarks and references to Appendices
Wezemaal-Belgium	1st		A wet day.	AHH
	2nd		Drill parade in morning	AHH
	3rd		Fine day. 3 O.R. to U.K. on leave	AHH
"	4th		Usual divine service parades	AHH
"	5th		Fine day. 1 Off. on leave in U.K. posted to 3/R.M.F. Struck off strength	AHH
"	6th		Drill parade. 1 O.R. to hospital	AHH
"	7th		Arr. mails of XIIIth Corps Group Packet arr. of E. of LE QUESNOY	AHH
"	8th		Inspection of cadre in marching order. 4 O.R. to U.K. on leave.	AHH
"	9th		Fine day. O.R. Sgt transferred with all records from 3rd Echelon G.H.Q. to Records Cork	AHH
"	10th		XIII Corps Groups Packet Shots to take place at Caudry. Strength 50 "Os" (Composed 3 Os)	AHH
"			2/RMF + 5 O.R. Hainslin Rgt.) won tug of war	AHH
"	11th		Fine day. Shower in afternoon. 2 O.R. returned from escort	AHH
"	12th		4 O.R. to Dist Reception Camp for disposal. W/m Officer reported.	AHH
			as follows: Struck off Strength Pt. Lieut T.W. Hayes to No. 346 P.o.W Coy	
			Lieut J.T. Shefeild to 167 P.o.W. Coy. Lieut R.C. Kent to 143 P.o.W Coy Kent	
			Pt. Ryan to 281 P.o.W. Coy. Lieut Pt. Crosby to 343 P.o.W. Coy. Lieut	
			P.V. Goodman (RAF ali/RMF) to U.K. on leave & to rejoin on return 250 P.o.W. Coy.	AHH

Secret

WO 52

War Diary

2nd Royal Munster Fusiliers

May 1916

2ND BATTALION,
ROYAL MUNSTER
FUSILIERS.
France
Date 31.5.16

2/Royal Munster Fusiliers

Army Form C. 2118.

WAR DIARY
or
INTELLIGENCE SUMMARY.
(Erase heading not required.)

Sheet 1

May 1919

Place	Date	Hour	Summary of Events and Information	Remarks and references to Appendices
Wimereux Pct	1st		A wet day	AAA
	2nd		Drill parade in morning	AAA
	3rd		Fine day. 3 O.R. to U.K. on leave	AAA
	4th		Usual divine service parade	AAA
	5th		Fine day. 1 O.R. on leave in U.K. posted to 3/R.M.F. Struck off strength	AAA
	6th		Drill parade. 1 O.R. to hospital	AAA
	7th		Draft tusk of XIII Corps Group Packet crews of E. of Le Quesnoy	AAA
	8th		Inspection of cadre in marching order. 4 O.R. to U.K. on leave	AAA
	9th		Fine day. O.R. Sgt transferred with all records from 3rd Echelon G.H.Q. to Records Cork	AAA
	10th		XIII Corps Group Packet Shots to take place at Caudry. Several 50 "D's" Kompanie 3 gt	AAA
			2/RMF + 5 O.R. Admin Staff were tug of war	AAA
	11th		Fine day. Shower in afternoon. 2 O.R. reported from escort	AAA
	12th		4 O.R. to First Reception Camp for disposal. W/M Officer reported	
			As follows Struck off Strength Lieut. T. W. Hayes to No. 344 P.o.W. Coy	
			Lieut J.T. Shekeld to 157 P.o.W. Coy. Lieut P.E. Kent to 143 P.o.W. Coy Lieut	
			P.J. Ryan to 281 P.o.W. Coy. Lieut P.J. Crosby to 343 P.o.W. Coy. Lieut	
			P.V. Goodman (R&f all H2RMF) to U.K. on leave + to rejoin on return 250 P.o.W. Coy.	AAA

WAR DIARY or INTELLIGENCE SUMMARY

Army Form C. 2118.

2/Royal Munster Fusiliers

Sheet No. 1

May 1919.

Place	Date	Hour	Summary of Events and Information	Remarks and references to Appendices
Wargnies-le-Petit	13.		2nd Lt. R. Morrissy C.F. proceeded to No. 3 Area on reposting - 3 O.R. to U.K. on leave	A.S.H.
"	14.		1. O.R. rejoined Battn. from Gen. Base Depôt - (Havre) - One O.R.	A.S.H.
"	15.		6 O.R. proceeded to Division reception Camp for Chigwell - 1st Freeman rejoined from leave U.K.	A.S.H.
"	16.		Fine day. C.O's inspection of G. Webb	1st F.S.M.
"	17.		Fine day - Capt. Gloster M.C. rejoined from leave of absence	A.S.H.
"	18.		1. O.R. to Divisional reception Camp for Chigwell. 4. O.R.S to U.K. on leave - 2/R.M.F. 2/Wilts & 2/Hinstin held a gymkhana in afternoon for entertainment of French population	A.S.H.
"	19.		Capt. I.F. Gloster M.C. proceeded on reposting to command 49 P.O.W. Coy. 2nd Lt. G.J. Freeman proceeded for duty with No. 250 P.O.W. Coy. - 1 O.R. rejoined from hospital	A.S.H.
"	20.		Fine day.	A.S.H.
"	21.		Fine day - Morning parade - Baths	A.S.H.
"	22.		Fine day. 1 O.R. (Pri Sumpany) reported from Cadre of 156 Bde H.Q.	A.S.H.
"	23.		2/Lt A.F. Burke reported for duty as Education Officer Avesnes Sub-area - (Cavalry Bde) CR 10284(0). Lt. Col B.N. Purdon M.C. proceeded on leave of absence to U.K. Command of Battn. assumed by Capt. F.A.S.F. McDowell M.C. - 3 O.R. to U.K. on leave.	A.S.H.

2/ Royal Munster Fusiliers

WAR DIARY
INTELLIGENCE SUMMARY.
Sheet 111   May 1919

Place	Date	Hour	Summary of Events and Information	Remarks and references to Appendices
Wargnies-le-Petit	24		3 O.R. rejoined from leave U.K.	A/A
"	25	0900	Sunday. Placed at disposal of Batn. Took a R.C. party to attend Requiem Mass and unveiling of memorial tablet to french soldiers at LE QUESNOY. The orderly room after two months occupation of Billet No 104 (Regt. No of 2nd Batn) was moved to Billet 101 (Regt No of 21st Batn).	A/A
"	26		Dull day. 4 O.R. rejoined from leave to U.K.	A/A
"	27		1 Offr (Capt W.J. Maguire MC) proceeded to U.K. on leave	A/A
"	28		4 O.R. to U.K. on leave. Practice fire drill in morning (evening).	A/A
"	29		1 O.R. proceeded for dispersal. Fine day.	A/A
"	30	1000	Fine day. Inspection of Cadre in marching order. Orders received for Cadre to entrain LE QUESNOY 2/6/19 thence proceed AINTREE	A/A
"	31		Friday. Lt. C.J. Ryan arrived to assist 2/Lt. P. Glen (Rtd) on completion of course at Oxford + Strath N. strength. 2. O.R. rejoined from leave of absence in U.K. Horses + mules Nil —	A/A

Strength at H.Q. 2 Officers, 23 O.R.
On leave   2 "   12 "
Detached   2 "   Nil "

H.S. Holt Captain
Cmdg 2/ Royal Munster [Fusiliers]

www.ingramcontent.com/pod-product-compliance
Lightning Source LLC
Chambersburg PA
CBHW081413160426

43193CB00013B/2164